CHRIS PENMAN

Fortress Facades

Protect, Prevent, Prosper – Strategies for Secure Commercial Properties

Copyright © 2024 by Chris Penman

©2024 Chris Penman. All rights reserved. No part of this publication may be reproduced, distributed, or transmitted in any form or by any means, including photocopying, recording, or other electronic or mechanical methods, without the prior written permission of the publisher, except in the case of brief quotations embodied in critical reviews and certain other noncommercial uses permitted by copyright law. For permission requests, write to the publisher at STARK Consulting Engineers.

The advice and strategies contained herein may not be suitable for every situation. This work is sold with the understanding that the author and publisher are not engaged in rendering legal, accounting, or other professional services. If professional assistance is required, the services of a competent professional should be sought. Neither the publisher nor the author shall be liable for damages arising here from. The fact that an organisation or website is referred to in this work as a citation and/or a potential source of further information does not mean that the author or the publisher endorses the information the organisation or website may provide or recommendations it may make. Further, readers should be aware that Internet websites listed in this work may have changed or disappeared between when this work was written and when it is read. No guarantee is given that the advice provided herein will result in successful outcomes. The publisher and author disclaim any liability, loss, or risk, personal or otherwise, which is incurred as a consequence, directly or indirectly, of the use and application of any of the contents of this book.

First edition

*This book was professionally typeset on Reedsy.
Find out more at reedsy.com*

Contents

IMPORTANT: READ THIS FIRST   v
INTRODUCTION   x

1   BULLETPROOF BEGINNINGS: UNDERSTANDING BULLETPROOF GLASS   1
    The Basics of Bulletproof Glass   1
    Design Principles for Bulletproof Glass   5
    Installation and Maintenance of Bulletproof Glass   8

2   FORTIFYING FACADES: ENHANCING STRUCTURAL INTEGRITY   14
    Understanding Facade Vulnerabilities   14
    Advanced Materials for Facades   18
    Design Strategies for Resilient Facades   21

3   BOLLARD BASICS: PERIMETER DEFENCE STRATEGIES   28
    Introduction to Bollards   28
    Placement and Layout of Bollards   33
    Beyond Bollards: Comprehensive Perimeter Security   36

4   INSIDE OUT SECURITY: SAFEGUARDING INTERIOR SPACES   43
    Critical Areas of Focus   43
    Interior Reinforcement Techniques   47
    Technology Integration for Internal Security   51

5 THE HUMAN FACTOR: TRAINING AND PREPAREDNESS 57
Creating a Security Culture 57
Emergency Response Planning 61
Continuity Planning for Business Operations 64

6 ASSESSING THREATS: UNDERSTANDING RISK 71
Types of Threats and Their Origins 71
Risk Assessment Methodologies 75
Implementing a Risk Management Plan 78

7 LEGAL AND COMPLIANCE CONSIDERATIONS 85
Building Regulations and Standards 85
Insurance and Liability 89
Ethics and Privacy Concerns 93

8 FUTURE-PROOFING: STAYING AHEAD OF THREATS 99
Emerging Threats and Technologies 99
Sustainable Security Solutions 103
Continuous Improvement and Adaptation 107

9 CASE STUDIES OF SECURED BUILDINGS 113
Lessons from the Front Lines 113
Innovations in Action 116
Global Examples of Excellence 120

10 BUILDING YOUR SECURITY BLUEPRINT 126
Planning and Designing for Security 126
Budgeting for Building Security 130
Implementing and Reviewing Security Measures 133

SECURING SUCCESS: EMBRACING THE FUTURE OF DEFENCE 140

IMPORTANT: READ THIS FIRST

Hi, I'm Chris Penman, and I'm grateful you took the opportunity to get this book. As a passionate expert with over 30 years in the industry of bulletproof and bomb blast-resistant building facade designs, I've encountered countless misconceptions and burning questions. It's these very challenges that have compelled me to compile the insights and strategies you'll find in " Fortress Facades: Protect, Prevent, Prosper," a guide aimed at transforming your approach to securing commercial properties.

Having spearheaded numerous projects across high-value sectors, I understand the intricacies of safeguarding assets and lives against unforeseen threats. The evolving landscape of security threats has only deepened my commitment to delivering state-of-the-art solutions that not only protect but also enhance the value of your properties.

After all, maybe you've felt the frustration of seeing your cutting-edge software development studio or prestigious legal firm vulnerable to attacks, despite previous investments in security. The fear that a single car bomb or backpack explosive could unravel years of hard work and put countless lives at risk is not just a theoretical risk but a daunting reality you've had to consider more seriously than ever.

Maybe you've experienced the confusion of navigating the myriad of options for facade security, each promising unmatched protection, yet none offering clear, proven results that align with your specific needs. The complexity of choosing the right solution can be overwhelming, leaving you uncertain if your investment will deliver the peace of mind and safety you desperately seek.

Or maybe you've even felt misled by security consultants who, despite their best intentions, have recommended systems that are either over-engineered or insufficient for the type of threats your building might face. This mismatch between threat assessment and solution can lead to not only wasted resources but also a false sense of security.

And look, I get it, it's not fair.

The truth is, you're not alone; it seems most are becoming victims of outdated or generalized approaches that fail to address the unique challenges faced by high-value industries. This common oversight can leave critical vulnerabilities unaddressed, putting your entire operation at risk.

That feeling of vulnerability, uncertainty, and frustration is something you know all too well. It gnaws at you each time you consider the safety of your team and the continuity of your operations. It's the sleepless nights wondering if you've done enough to protect everything you've worked so hard to build.

Here's what most don't realise: the conventional security measures often do not account for the sophisticated and ever-evolving nature of modern threats. The landscape of aggression has transformed, requiring a nuanced and dynamic approach to protection that many existing systems fail to provide.

And now with the possibility of increased threats in urban centres, the urgency for tailored, robust security solutions is more pressing than ever. It's no longer just about preventing damage; it's about ensuring resilience, maintaining operations, and safeguarding your reputation amidst potential crises.

It seems most are left in a state of reactive panic post-incident, scrambling to implement measures that could have mitigated damage or even prevented the attack. The real fear lies in the aftermath—how it impacts your business continuity, the psychological effect on your staff, and the potential irreversible damage to your brand's trust and client loyalty.

The Perpetual Loop of Vulnerability

In the world of high-value commercial property ownership, there exists a relentless cycle that seems almost impossible to escape—the Perpetual Loop of Vulnerability. You, as an owner of such properties, might find this loop all too familiar. It is a cycle of concern, trial, error, temporary relief, and eventual disappointment. Let's walk through each step to truly understand the mechanics of this frustrating loop.

Awareness Perhaps you've recently read about an incident, or worse, experienced a close call yourself. The reality of the threat hits you hard. It's no longer about 'if' but 'when'. The safety of your building and the people within it becomes a pressing concern. You start to imagine the catastrophic effects of a car bomb or a backpack explosive. This heightened awareness is the first step, a trigger that propels you into action.

Reaction Driven by the initial shock, you react. Maybe you hire more security personnel, install conventional security cameras, or introduce strict access controls. It feels good to take action, to see tangible security measures being put in place. You tell yourself that these steps will deter or mitigate any potential threats. However, deep down, there's a nagging feeling that these are just surface-level solutions.

Frustration As time passes, the effectiveness of your new security measures starts to wane. Maybe your staff finds the increased security measures cumbersome, impacting their daily activities, or perhaps you notice that these conventional methods are not as foolproof as hoped. The initial confidence in your reactive measures begins to crumble, leading to frustration. This frustration grows as you realize that despite your efforts and investment, the fundamental vulnerabilities remain.

Illusion of Safety In an effort to quell your fears and frustration, you might decide to adopt a few more advanced technologies or strategies, ones that promise better results. For a moment, it seems like you've finally secured your property. There's a brief period where everything seems under control; your tenants feel safe, and so do you. This illusion of safety is comforting but, unfortunately, it's just that—an illusion.

Disillusionment Eventually, the reality shatters your temporary peace. Perhaps there's another incident nearby or a security test fails. Suddenly, the cycle is set to repeat. The measures you thought would protect your property seem inadequate once more. This realization is disheartening, and you find yourself back at square one, faced again with the critical need for a truly effective solution.

It just goes to show that doing the same things and expecting different results might lead you into a continuous loop of vulnerability. It would be wise to consider a fundamentally different approach to secure your property and safeguard the people within from severe threats like car bombs and backpack explosives, thus stopping this cycle of pain and frustration.

Which is why I'm glad you're reading this book. As you turn the page and start reading, you will finally gain the insights and answers you've been seeking. This knowledge will empower you to break free from the Perpetual Loop of Vulnerability and move towards a genuinely secure future for your commercial property.

INTRODUCTION

Imagine a fortress. Not the kind from ancient history books, standing solitary amidst a wild, untamed landscape, but a modern-day commercial stronghold nestled right in the heart of bustling cityscapes. This fortress, your building, houses not soldiers but some of the brightest minds in software development, legal counselling, accounting, and other high-value industries. The treasure trove wthin isn't gold or jewels—it's intellectual property, sensitive data, innovative projects, and influential connections. The question is, how well protected is your fortress?

In the dynamic world of commercial property ownership, the notion of security extends far beyond locks and keys. It's about crafting an environment that not only safeguards against external threats but also enhances the productivity and wellbeing of those within its walls. This isn't just about protection; it's about creating a bastion where businesses can thrive unimpeded by the fear of disruption.

Part One: The Significance of a Secure Foundation

Security is an investment in your business's future. In the same way that you wouldn't leave your doors unlocked overnight, turning a blind eye to the broader aspects of security in today's hyper-connected world can leave your business vulnerable. The implications of a breach are not just financial; they can destabilise your business, erode trust with your clients, and even jeopardise future growth. However, with the right strategies, the story can be very different.

Consider how a well-fortified environment can transform your business operations. It's about more than just deterring theft or vandalism; it's about creating a space that fosters innovation by ensuring that the brightest minds working under your roof feel secure and valued. When employees are confident in their physical and digital safety, their focus shifts entirely towards innovation and productivity. Security, therefore, is not just a preventative measure; it is a catalyst for growth and prosperity.

Part Two: The Holistic Approach to Security

Achieving comprehensive security is akin to assembling a complex puzzle. Every piece, whether it's bulletproof glass, fortified structures, strategic entry points, or advanced surveillance, plays a crucial role. However, it isn't just about the physical and technological defences you install. Human factors, such as employee training and preparedness, are equally pivotal. Your staff should be your first line of defence, not your weakest link.

Moreover, understanding the landscape of threats helps in crafting strategies that are not merely reactive but are anticipatory and adaptive. The legal and compliance considerations tied to your industry's specific needs also play a crucial role in shaping your security protocols. Ignorance of these aspects can lead to vulnerabilities that are as dangerous as leaving your front door unlocked.

Future-proofing your security isn't just a one-time project; it's an ongoing journey. As threats evolve, so must your strategies. Staying ahead means being proactive, innovative, and continually reassessing your security posture in response to emerging risks. This forward-thinking approach ensures that your commercial property remains a fortress, impervious to the threats of both today and tomorrow.

Part Three: Empowering Your Security Blueprint

The final piece of the puzzle is implementation. Knowing what to do is only as good as doing it effectively. This book aims to serve as your blueprint, guiding you through each step of evaluating, enhancing, and maintaining the security of your commercial property. From the physical structure of your building to the resilience of your operational processes, every aspect of your security plan should align with the overarching goal of not just preventing loss but enabling prosperity.

Each chapter of this book is designed to address specific components of security, tailored for high-stakes industries like yours. By integrating these principles, you will not only protect your assets but also position your business as a secure, reliable, and forward-thinking establishment—qualities that are invaluable in today's competitive market.

As you turn these pages, think of each chapter as a layer of defence, each section a building block towards a more secure and productive future. Remember, the goal isn't just to protect—it's to enable your business to reach its fullest potential, unhampered by threats and secure in its fortifications. Let's embark on this journey to transform your commercial property into a true modern-day fortress, where you can protect, prevent, and most importantly, prosper.

Welcome to " Fortress Facades: Protect, Prevent, Prosper - Strategies for Secure Commercial Properties." Your blueprint to a safer, more resilient commercial space starts here.

1

BULLETPROOF BEGINNINGS: UNDERSTANDING BULLETPROOF GLASS

"Safety is a cheap and effective insurance policy." - **Author Unknown**

The Basics of Bulletproof Glass

When you're in the business of safeguarding assets as critical as software code, legal documents, or financial records, the integrity of your commercial property's security measures must be nothing short of top-notch. That's where bulletproof glass comes into play. It's not just a feature of spy movies; it's a real-world necessity for high-stakes industries like yours. Let's dive into what bulletproof glass is made of, the different levels of bullet resistance it offers, and the standards and certifications you should be aware of before making an investment.

Composition and Materials

At first glance, bulletproof glass might look similar to the ordinary glass adorning storefronts or office buildings, but its internal makeup is much more complex and fascinating. Technically referred to as bullet-resistant glass because it's designed to resist bullets rather than be entirely bulletproof, this material is a lifesaver in literal terms.

The core materials involved in the manufacture of bulletproof glass are typically a combination of two primary elements: polycarbonate and laminated glass. Laminated glass alone consists of layers of glass sheets bonded together with polyvinyl butyral (PVB) or ethylene-vinyl acetate (EVA). When a bullet strikes this type of glass, the outer layer might shatter, but the plastic interlayer absorbs and redistributes the energy of the bullet, preventing it from penetrating through.

Polycarbonate, a type of strong, durable plastic, is added to the laminate layers to make the glass even more resistant. The polycarbonate layer is usually the final layer facing the interior of a building, acting as a catch-all for any fragments or residual force from a bullet impact. This layering not only prevents penetration but also reduces the risk of spalling — where shards from the glass could fly off and cause injury to people inside.

Levels of Bullet Resistance

Understanding the levels of bullet resistance is crucial for you when choosing the right type of bulletproof glass. The resistance levels are determined by the ability of the glass to withstand the impact of bullets of various sizes and speeds. These levels are categorised largely by standards set by certifying bodies, which we will discuss shortly.

Generally, bullet resistance levels are classified from BR1 to BR7, with BR1 being the least resistant and BR7 the most. For example, BR1-rated glass can stop three rounds from a 9mm handgun, which might be adequate for low-risk environments. On the other hand, BR6-rated glass can withstand multiple rounds from a high-calibre assault rifle, which would be appropriate for buildings at higher risk of violent attacks.

Choosing the right level depends greatly on the specific threats you perceive to your property. For instance, if you're running a software game development company with highly valuable intellectual property, opting for a higher level of bullet resistance might be a prudent decision.

Standards and Certifications

When you're investing in bullet-resistant glass, it's not just about picking the thickest pane you can find. Compliance with recognised standards and certifications is crucial to ensure that the product you're installing has been rigorously tested and proven effective under specified conditions.

In Europe, the standard to look out for is the EN1063 standard. It details specifications for testing and classification of bullet resistance in glass. This standard defines the type of firearms and bullets used in the testing process, ensuring that the glass meets a minimum safety threshold when faced with real-world threats.

Another important certification is from the Underwriters Laboratories (UL) in the United States, particularly the UL752 standard. Similar to EN1063, UL752 outlines different levels of protection, specifying the type of firearms and ammunition that the glass must withstand to meet each level of certification.

Ensuring that your chosen bulletproof glass meets these standards is not just about ticking a box. It's about reassurance that the product will perform as expected in the unfortunate event of an armed attack. It's also a signal to your clients, your employees, and yourself that you take security seriously and are proactive about protecting your business's valuable assets.

In choosing bulletproof glass, understanding its composition, the levels of resistance it offers, and the relevant standards and certifications is paramount. This knowledge not only helps in making an informed purchasing decision but also sets the foundation for a secure, resilient commercial environment where you can focus on what you do best — innovate and lead in your industry.

Design Principles for Bulletproof Glass

Balancing Transparency and Security

When you're fortifying your commercial property with bulletproof glass, one of your primary concerns might be maintaining a welcoming, transparent aesthetic without compromising on security. This balance is crucial, especially in industries like software development, legal services, and accountancy, where professionalism and openness need to blend seamlessly with safety measures.

The transparency of bulletproof glass is generally dictated by its thickness and the materials used in its composition. Typically, the glass is made by layering a combination of polycarbonate (plastic) and glass to create a robust barrier. The more layers, the higher the bullet resistance, but this also affects the clarity of the glass. Advanced manufacturing techniques now allow for high levels of transparency even in thicker glass, which is essential for storefronts or buildings where aesthetic considerations are just as important as security.

To achieve the perfect balance, consider the specific threats or risks in your area. For example, a software game developer in a metropolitan area might face different security risks compared to a rural legal practice. Assessing these risks with a security consultant can help you decide the level of bullet resistance needed without overinvesting in unnecessarily thick or visually obstructive glass.

Moreover, the use of coatings can enhance both the bullet resistance and the clarity of the glass. Some coatings can reduce glare and UV exposure, which not only protects against bullets but also enhances the working environment inside the building by reducing eye strain and exposure to harmful rays.

Frame Design Considerations

The frame that holds your bulletproof glass is as crucial as the glass itself. A robust frame must support the weight and impact resistance of bulletproof glass, which is significantly heavier than standard glass. Aluminium frames are commonly used due to their strength-to-weight ratio, corrosion resistance, and the ability to be fashioned into aesthetically pleasing designs.

However, the design of the frame goes beyond material choice. The way a frame is constructed and integrated into your building's architecture can impact its performance in a ballistic event. For instance, ensuring that there are no weak points or gaps in the frame that could be exploited by intruders is vital. Interlocking designs, where the frame pieces connect at each joint more securely, can provide additional resistance against forced entry.

In addition, consider the interior design implications of your frame choice. A bulky frame might provide high levels of security but could detract from the glass's transparency and the overall lightness of the architecture. Slimmer frames can be reinforced internally to provide security without compromising on style, especially important in high-value industries where client perception can influence business success.

Innovations in Bulletproof Glass Technology

The field of bulletproof glass is continuously evolving, with innovations that enhance both functionality and aesthetic appeal. One of the most exciting advancements is the development of smart bulletproof glass. This technology involves integrating electronic components within the glass to provide additional functionalities like opacity control or threat-level detection.

Opacity control allows you to switch the transparency of the glass. This can be particularly useful in scenarios where privacy is needed momentarily—think of a high-stakes meeting in a law firm or an accountant handling sensitive documents. At the flick of a switch, the glass can turn opaque, providing instant privacy without the need for cumbersome window treatments.

Threat-level detection technologies embedded within the glass can alert you to potential breaches or attempted break-ins. Some smart glasses are equipped with sensors that detect the force of an impact or the acoustic signature of a bullet, instantly triggering an alarm system and locking down the building if needed.

Such innovative technologies not only bolster security but also enhance the functionality of your space, adapting to different needs without manual intervention. While the upfront cost might be higher, the investment in smart bulletproof glass could provide long-term savings and advantages, particularly in terms of operational efficiencies and enhanced protective measures.

Incorporating bulletproof glass into your commercial property does not mean compromising on design or cutting-edge technology. By understanding and applying these principles of design, frame considerations, and embracing innovations, you can create a secure yet aesthetically appealing environment that protects and enhances your business operations.

Installation and Maintenance of Bulletproof Glass

Effective Installation Techniques

Getting bulletproof glass up and standing isn't just about plugging a super tough material into a window frame and calling it a day. It's an art—a meticulous process that demands precision to ensure that the security it promises is fully realised.

First off, choosing the right contractor can make or break the effectiveness of your bulletproof glass installation. You want a team that's not just skilled but experienced in handling high-security installations. Look for contractors with specific experience in commercial security installations, and don't shy away from requesting case studies or references. The nuances of bullet-resistant materials are many, and the installation process is as crucial as the manufacturing of the glass itself.

The frame that holds the glass is equally vital. Opt for materials that complement the strength of the bulletproof glass. Often, reinforced steel or similarly robust metals are used to match the durability and resistance level of the glass. The adhesion process also needs special care; using subpar bonding agents can weaken the installation, leaving potential vulnerabilities. Ensure that the sealants and fixatives used are of the highest quality and are applied generously to prevent any gaps.

Alignment is another critical factor. Even a slight misalignment during installation can lead to undue stress on the glass, potentially compromising its integrity and performance. Each pane should be meticulously measured and installed to ensure it fits perfectly within its frame.

Lastly, consider the broader architectural elements. Bulletproof glass is heavier than standard glass. Ensure that the supporting structure can handle the additional weight without compromising the building's structural integrity. This might involve reinforcing existing walls or installing new structural elements to support the weight.

Maintenance Best Practices

Once installed, bulletproof glass does require ongoing maintenance to ensure it retains its integrity and functionality. Neglect could lead to deterioration, which might not be immediately apparent but could severely undermine its protective qualities when you most need them.

Regular cleaning is essential, but it's not just about aesthetics. Use cleaning solutions that are specifically designed for use on bulletproof glass. Harsh chemicals can gradually erode the surface, making the glass more susceptible to damage over time. Typically, a solution of mild soap and warm water, applied with a soft, non-abrasive cloth, is effective enough. Avoid abrasive pads or brushes, as these can scratch the surface, potentially weakening its structural integrity.

Inspections should be part of your routine maintenance. Look for any signs of wear and tear such as chips, cracks, or even slight discolorations, which could indicate internal damage. If you spot any damage, no matter how minimal it appears, consult with a professional immediately. Bulletproof glass is designed to withstand multiple impacts, but its resistance can be compromised by visible damage.

The seals and frames should also be checked regularly. Environmental factors like temperature changes and humidity can cause materials to expand and contract, which might lead to gaps or weakening of the seals. Make sure that the frames and seals are inspected and maintained regularly to ensure that they continue to provide optimal support to the bulletproof glass panels.

Longevity and Durability Factors

The lifespan of bulletproof glass can be significantly enhanced with the right practices. Environmental factors play a huge role here. For instance, prolonged exposure to harsh sunlight can lead to delamination, which is when the layers of the glass begin to separate and thus weaken. Using window films can mitigate some of these effects by blocking out harmful UV rays.

The location of the installation also influences longevity. Glass installed in areas with high criminal activity or frequent violent weather conditions might endure more frequent impacts, necessitating more regular checks and potentially earlier replacement.

Technological advances have also introduced self-healing bulletproof glass, which contains a layer that can partially repair small cracks itself. While more expensive, investing in such innovations could reduce long-term maintenance costs and enhance the durability of your installation.

Remember, bulletproof glass is an investment in safety and security. With proper installation and diligent maintenance, it not only protects physical assets but also provides peace of mind, knowing that your premises are well-shielded against potential threats. Each minute spent on ensuring its optimal performance is a minute invested in safeguarding the future of your business.

RECAP AND ACTION ITEMS

Congratulations on making it through the in-depth exploration of bulletproof glass. Armed with this knowledge, you're now better equipped to fortify your commercial properties against potential threats, ensuring the safety of your assets and personnel.

Starting with the fundamentals, you've learned about the composition and materials that make glass bulletproof, the various levels of bullet resistance, and the critical standards and certifications that guide quality and effectiveness.

In terms of design, we delved into how to balance transparency with security — crucial for maintaining aesthetic value while protecting your premises. Additionally, you explored frame design considerations, which are just as vital as the glass itself in ensuring the effectiveness of your security measures. The innovations in bulletproof glass technology section opened your eyes to the advancements that can further enhance security without compromising on design.

Finally, the installation and maintenance segment equipped you with the knowledge to ensure that your bulletproof glass is installed correctly and maintained effectively, thereby extending its longevity and performance.

Here's what you should do next:

1. Assess Your Current Security Setup: Review your existing security measures and identify areas where bulletproof glass could provide significant benefits. Consider areas that are vulnerable or have high foot traffic.

2. Consult with Experts: Reach out to professionals who specialise in high-security installations. They can provide personalised insights and recommendations tailored to your specific needs and building specifications.

3. Plan Your Budget: Implementing bulletproof glass is an investment. Plan your finances accordingly, considering not only the initial installation but also long-term maintenance.

4. Stay Updated on Innovations: The field of security technology evolves rapidly. Keep yourself informed about new developments in bulletproof glass technology that might offer better protection or efficiency.

5. Schedule Regular Maintenance: Set up a routine maintenance schedule to ensure that your bulletproof installations continue to function optimally. Regular checks can often prevent minor issues from turning into major security vulnerabilities.

By taking these steps, you'll enhance the security of your premises significantly, giving you peace of mind and safeguarding your valuable assets. Remember, the safety you secure today is the prosperity you enjoy tomorrow.

2

FORTIFYING FACADES: ENHANCING STRUCTURAL INTEGRITY

"Strength does not come from physical capacity. It comes from an indomitable will." - Mahatma Gandhi

Understanding Facade Vulnerabilities

When it comes to commercial properties, the facade isn't just about kerb appeal—it's your first line of defence. Whether you're housing cutting-edge software development, intricate legal documents, or sensitive financial data, understanding where your building might be most vulnerable can make all the difference in enhancing its security and resilience. Let's delve into the aspects that every high-value industry property owner should be aware of.

Common weak points in building exteriors

The exterior of a building, particularly in commercial settings, is more than just a shell. It is a complex interface with the environment that can have several points of vulnerability, each posing unique threats. Windows, doors, and other openings are perhaps the most evident; these are necessary for functionality and comfort but represent clear entry points for both environmental hazards and malicious attacks.

Ventilation systems, while essential, can also offer access points that are less obvious but equally exploitable. The materials used in these areas might not always boast the strength and durability needed to withstand concerted efforts to breach them. It's crucial to assess not just the quality of the materials but also the design and integration of these systems.

Moreover, the junctions where different materials meet, such as where glass interfaces with metal or where the roof connects to the walls, can be potential weak spots. These areas often suffer from differential movements due to thermal expansion or contraction, potentially leading to gaps or weaknesses over time.

Impact of explosive forces on facades

Understanding the impact of explosive forces might not be pleasant, but it's essential. Explosive events, whether accidental or deliberate, exert a tremendous amount of pressure on building facades. The primary wave of an explosion hits a building's exterior with high-speed pressure, testing the integrity of materials and the construction's overall design.

The type of damage can vary significantly depending on the facade's materials and construction. For instance, glass, while aesthetically pleasing, is highly susceptible to shattering under blast pressures, creating potentially lethal shards. Solid walls might withstand the initial blast wave but can suffer from structural cracking, leading to long-term stability issues.

One of the critical aspects to consider is the facade's ability to dissipate energy. Designs that allow for some 'give' or flexibility can reduce the impact force's direct transmission through the structure, potentially saving the building from more severe damage.

Historical vulnerabilities and lessons learnt

History is laden with lessons on what not to do when it comes to facade design in high-stakes environments. Take, for example, the 1995 Oklahoma City bombing in the United States. The Alfred P. Murrah Federal Building's facade was not designed to handle such an assault and the devastation was profound. The attack led to a significant re-evaluation of how buildings should be constructed to handle such forces.

Across the pond, the 1996 Manchester bombing showed similar

lessons. The city's infrastructure suffered immensely because of vulnerabilities in facade designs that could not withstand the blast, leading to widespread damage and a long, costly rebuilding process.

From these and other similar incidents, several key lessons have emerged. Firstly, the importance of using robust, resilient materials cannot be overstated. Secondly, there is a critical need for comprehensive threat assessments during the design phase of building projects. Lastly, incorporating redundancy in the design can prevent total facade failure, allowing the structure to preserve its core integrity even under attack.

By examining these historical precedents, you can avoid the pitfalls of the past and fortify your property against potential threats. Understanding where weaknesses lie and how they can be exploited or damaged is crucial in designing a commercial facade that not only looks good but also offers the best protection possible.

In addressing facade vulnerabilities, you're not just putting up walls; you're strategising a fortress. Each decision in materials and design isn't just about aesthetics or cost—it's a calculated step towards safeguarding your assets, your data, and your people. As we move forward, keep these vulnerabilities in mind; they are the chinks in your armour that need the most attention and thoughtful intervention.

Advanced Materials for Facades

When you're considering the safety and security of your commercial property, the choice of materials for your building's facade is not just about aesthetics but also about resilience and functionality. The facade is your first line of defence against external threats, be they environmental or man-made. With the advent of modern materials and technologies, the scope for enhancing the structural integrity of commercial properties has broadened. Let's dive into what these materials are, how they compare with traditional choices, and what kind of cost-benefit analysis might make sense for high-stakes businesses like yours.

Modern Materials and Technologies

The landscape of facade materials has evolved dramatically. Gone are the days when choices were limited to concrete, brick, and glass. Today, you can select from a variety of advanced materials that offer enhanced protective qualities without compromising on design.

One standout is High-Performance Concrete (HPC). This isn't your average concrete; it's engineered for extreme durability and tensile strength, thanks to the incorporation of fine particles and specific admixtures. It's particularly effective in environments that demand high impact resistance and longevity.

Then there's Blast-Resistant Glass. Traditional glass shatters upon impact, posing a hazard. Blast-resistant glass, typically made using multiple layers bonded with plastic interlayers, is designed to withstand explosions, ensuring the glass remains intact or stays in place even when broken.

Metal mesh is another innovative option. Stainless steel or aluminium meshes can be incorporated into the glass panels of facades. This not only adds an extra layer of security but also provides a unique aesthetic that can be customised to your liking.

Emerging too are smart materials like Shape Memory Alloys (SMA) and Piezoelectric materials. SMAs have the ability to return to their original shape after deformation, offering exceptional resilience. Piezoelectric materials, on the other hand, can generate an electric charge in response to applied mechanical stress, potentially playing a role in sensing and mitigating stress on building facades.

Comparing Traditional vs. Advanced Materials

While traditional materials like brick and mortar have stood the test of time for reliability, they often fall short when it comes to handling modern security threats like blasts or severe weather impacts. Traditional materials typically have a lower initial cost but might not always provide the best long-term value, especially in high-risk scenarios your business might face.

Advanced materials, while often more expensive upfront, bring significant advantages. Take HPC and blast-resistant glass; their enhanced durability and resilience can drastically reduce the likelihood of extensive damage during events like urban explosions, which are a realistic threat for high-profile industries. This means potentially lower repair costs and less downtime for your business — an essential factor when every minute of productivity counts.

Moreover, advanced materials can be engineered to specific requirements. This means they can be tailored not just for performance but also for aesthetics, thus maintaining the architectural integrity and appeal of your property — a crucial consideration in sectors where brand image is tightly linked to physical presence.

Cost-Benefit Analysis of Facade Materials

Deciding on materials for your facade involves weighing the initial costs against long-term benefits. Here's where a detailed cost-benefit analysis comes into play. This analysis should consider not only the direct costs, such as material and installation expenses, but also indirect costs like maintenance, durability, and even insurance premiums, which can vary significantly based on the assessed risk of the building.

Advanced materials, although initially more costly, could result in lower overall expenditures in the form of reduced maintenance needs and lesser frequency of replacements. For example, the investment in blast-resistant glass could prevent a scenario where a single incident causes extensive glass damage, thereby not only saving on immediate repair costs but also potentially reducing hike in insurance rates due to increased risk factors.

Furthermore, the choice of advanced materials could boost your building's value. Properties equipped with state-of-the-art materials that enhance safety and durability are often more appealing to potential buyers and tenants, reflecting a forward-thinking asset management approach.

In conclusion, as you consider the various materials available for your commercial property's facade, think beyond the initial expense. Evaluate how these choices align with your broader business objectives — including safety, durability, aesthetics, and financial prudence. Whether it's opting for high-performance concrete or integrating cutting-edge smart materials, your focus should be on securing a facade that not only protects but also adds long-term value to your property. Remember, in high-value industries, the right facade can be more than just a shell; it can be a strategic asset.

Design Strategies for Resilient Facades

Integrating Flexibility in Building Design

When you think about building design, flexibility might not be the first word that springs to mind, especially in the context of structural security. However, the ability to adapt and withstand external pressures is a key component in modern architecture, particularly for commercial properties in high-stakes industries. Flexibility in building design doesn't just refer to the physical bending of materials but also to the capacity of a building to absorb, adapt, and recover from disruptive events, such as explosions or natural disasters.

Incorporating elements such as base isolation systems, which enable a building to move independently of its foundation, can significantly reduce the risk of structural damage during an earthquake. Similarly, the use of flexible joint connectors in your building's design allows for slight movements and adjustments during high wind loads or seismic activities. These technologies are designed to bear a significant amount of stress, protecting the building's integrity and, crucially, the people and valuable assets inside.

Think of it like designing a building that can dance with the environment instead of standing rigid against it. This approach not only enhances the lifespan of your property but also significantly reduces maintenance costs over time. For high-value industries, where downtime can result in substantial financial losses, ensuring minimal operational disruptions is a must.

Blast-Resistant Design Features

Blast resistance might sound like a feature reserved for military installations, but in an era where security threats are increasingly unpredictable, it has become a pertinent aspect of commercial property design. Integrating blast-resistant features into the facade of your building is not about expecting the worst but ensuring a level of preparedness that maintains security and peace of mind.

One of the most effective strategies is the use of blast-resistant glazing. Traditional windows are often the weakest point in a building's exterior; however, by implementing windows designed to resist shattering upon impact, you can drastically enhance the safety of your building's interior. These specialised windows are typically made from laminated glass, consisting of multiple layers bonded with interlayers of polyvinyl butyral (PVB) or ethylene-vinyl acetate (EVA). In the event of a blast, these windows are designed to hold together, significantly reducing the risk of injury from flying glass shards.

Another key feature is the reinforcement of facades using ultra-high performance concrete (UHPC). This material offers superior strength and durability compared to standard concrete and is particularly adept at absorbing energy from blasts. When used in exterior walls, UHPC can help prevent structural collapse, providing crucial extra minutes for evacuation and emergency response.

The perimeter of your building should also be considered as part of your blast-resistant strategy. The use of bollards, barriers, and landscaped terraces can serve as both aesthetic features and protective barriers, capable of absorbing and dissipating energy from potential explosions before they reach your building.

Aesthetic Considerations in Secure Facade Design

Now, let's talk aesthetics. It's vital to remember that securing your building doesn't have to mean compromising on design. In fact, the challenge of integrating high-security features with eye-catching design can result in truly innovative architecture that stands out from the crowd — for all the right reasons.

Material choice plays a pivotal role here. For instance, the use of textured concrete panels not only adds an element of visual interest but can also be configured to enhance blast resistance. Similarly, metal facades can offer a sleek, modern look while providing substantial durability and protection. The key is to work with materials that are both functional and visually appealing, ensuring that your building remains welcoming and attractive while being securely fortified.

Incorporating green spaces and natural elements into your facade design can also enhance aesthetic appeal while contributing to security. Strategic placement of trees, shrubs, and other landscaping features can provide a natural barrier against external threats, all while promoting a more pleasant and productive environment for occupants.

Lastly, consider the psychological impact of design. A building that appears fortress-like can be intimidating and unwelcoming, potentially deterring clients and visitors. By integrating security features seamlessly into the design, such that they enhance rather than dominate the building's appearance, you create a space that feels safe and inviting rather than oppressive.

In sum, designing resilient facades requires a balance of flexibility, strength, and aesthetics. By considering each of these elements in your approach, you can ensure your property not only stands the test of time but does so with style, all while providing the highest level of security for your high-value operations. This strategic blend of design innovation and technical resilience is what will set your commercial property apart in any high-stakes industry.

RECAP AND ACTION ITEMS

As you've explored the intricacies of fortifying your commercial property's facade, you now stand at a crucial juncture where understanding, planning, and action converge. You've delved into the common vulnerabilities that can turn a building's exterior into a liability, recognised the potential devastation caused by explosive forces, and drawn lessons from historical precedents. Knowledge, as they say, is power, but only when it's applied.

Moving forward, you've also gained insight into the world of advanced materials and technologies that can significantly enhance the structural integrity of your buildings. By comparing these with traditional materials, you have a clearer picture of what modern solutions can offer and the cost implications associated with upgrading. Remember, investing in high-quality materials not only increases security but also adds to the long-term value of your property.

Moreover, integrating strategic design elements into your building can make a significant difference in its resilience. Flexible design approaches and blast-resistant features are no longer just optional; they're essential components of modern commercial architecture, especially in high-stakes industries like yours. Additionally, while focusing on security, you've also considered the aesthetic aspect of facade design to ensure that the building remains welcoming and visually appealing.

Here are actionable steps you can take to enhance the safety and integrity of your commercial properties:

1. Assess Your Current Vulnerabilities: Hire a professional to conduct a thorough assessment of your building's facades. Identify the weak points and prioritise them based on the level of risk they present.

2. Consult with Experts: Engage with architects and engineers who specialise in secure building designs. Their expertise will be invaluable in integrating advanced materials and blast-resistant features into your existing properties.

3. Invest in Advanced Materials: Allocate budget towards upgrading to more resilient materials. While the initial costs may be higher, the long-term benefits in terms of security and durability often justify the investment.

4. Plan for Aesthetics: Work with designers to ensure that security enhancements align with the overall aesthetic goals of your property. Secure doesn't have to mean stark or uninviting.

5. Educate Your Team: Ensure that everyone involved in your property management understands the new features and materials. Knowledge about why these changes are essential will foster a better appreciation and upkeep of the security measures.

6. Review Regularly: Security is not a one-time effort but an ongoing process. Regularly review and update your security measures to adapt to evolving threats and new advancements in technology.

By acting on these steps, you not only protect your assets but also enhance the working environment for everyone using the building. Remember, a fortified facade is your first line of defence in preserving the integrity and prosperity of your business.

3

BOLLARD BASICS: PERIMETER DEFENCE STRATEGIES

"The true art of defence is not to be too much on your guard." - *Alexander Pope*

Introduction to Bollards

When it comes to securing your commercial property, every detail counts, especially in high-value industries like software game development, legal practices, and accounting. An often-overlooked aspect of physical security is the humble bollard: those sturdy, short posts that guide traffic and protect pedestrians and properties from vehicle intrusions. But there's much more to bollards than meets the eye. Let's dive into the world of bollards to understand their types, materials, and the balance between aesthetics and function.

Types of Bollards

Bollards come in various shapes and sizes, each designed with specific purposes in mind. Understanding these can help you choose the right type that best fits your security needs and aesthetic preferences.

1. Fixed Bollards: These are permanently installed into the ground. They provide a high level of security and are ideal for protecting sensitive areas where vehicular access should be strictly controlled or prohibited. They're a common sight around government buildings or high-profile company headquarters.

2. Retractable Bollards: These are designed to rise or retract into the ground, allowing temporary access when needed. They are perfect for areas that require occasional vehicle access, such as service entrances or emergency routes.

3. Removable Bollards: Similar to retractable ones but manually removed and replaced. These are suitable for locations where access needs change frequently but do not justify the cost of fully automated systems.

4. Flexible Bollards: Made from materials that bend upon impact, these bollards are less about stopping vehicles and more about warning drivers or delineating traffic paths. They're commonly used in car parks or mixed-use spaces where pedestrian safety is a priority, but vehicle access is still necessary.

5. Decorative Bollards: While they offer some level of protection, their primary focus is on aesthetics, enhancing the visual appeal of the landscape while offering moderate security.

Choosing the right type of bollard depends on your specific security needs, operational requirements, and budget. For instance, if you run a software development company housed in a facility with a high risk of industrial espionage, investing in retractable bollards might be wise to control access without compromising on emergency egress needs.

Material Choices for Bollards

The material of a bollard determines its strength, durability, maintenance needs, and aesthetic appeal. Here's a rundown of common materials used in bollard construction:

1. Steel: Highly durable and strong, steel bollards are capable of withstanding significant impact. They are ideal for high-security areas. Stainless steel variants offer added resistance to rust and corrosion, making them suitable for properties in harsh weather environments.

2. Concrete: Offering robust protection, concrete bollards are often used where a permanent, immovable barrier is needed. They can be finished with various textures or colours and double as decorative elements.

3. Aluminium: Lighter than steel and naturally resistant to corrosion, aluminium bollards are easier to install and relocate if necessary. However, they offer less impact resistance and are more suited to traffic control than outright security.

4. Plastic and Polyurethane: These materials are typically used for flexible or decorative bollards. They can be designed to look like other more robust materials but are primarily for visual deterrence and traffic management.

5. Wood: Wooden bollards can blend seamlessly into natural surroundings or historic areas where maintaining visual integrity is crucial. However, they require regular maintenance and are less durable against impacts.

The choice of material often hinges on the balance between security requirements and aesthetic considerations, which brings us to our next point.

Aesthetics vs. Function

For commercial properties, particularly in high-value sectors, the line between aesthetics and function is often blurred. You want a bollard that does its job—protecting your assets—but also one that fits seamlessly into the architectural and cultural context of your property.

Incorporating bollards should not feel like a compromise between safety and style. Today's market offers options that serve both purposes elegantly. For example, designer bollards with intricate patterns or custom colours can complement your building's exterior while providing the necessary perimeter security.

When planning the installation, consider how the bollards will look during different times of the day and in various weather conditions. The reflection of metal surfaces, the texture of concrete under different lights, and even the way shadows play around the bollards can all impact the perception of your property's facade.

Moreover, remember that the function extends beyond stopping vehicles; it includes guiding foot traffic, demarcating private spaces, and even acting as a psychological deterrent against unauthorised access. Each aspect needs to be thoughtfully integrated to create a secure yet welcoming environment for clients and employees alike.

In essence, choosing the right bollards for your property is a multifaceted decision. It requires a thorough understanding of your security needs, a keen eye for design, and a strategic approach to property management. Whether you are fortifying a game development studio against industrial espionage or a legal firm against potential threats, the correct use of bollards can significantly enhance your security posture without sacrificing aesthetic appeal.

Placement and Layout of Bollards

When it comes to securing your commercial property, the placement and layout of bollards play a pivotal role. They're not just metal posts plonked in the ground; they are strategic assets that need careful consideration to maximise their effectiveness. Whether you're protecting high-end software development studios, bustling legal practices, or confidential accounting firms, understanding the nuances of bollard placement can significantly enhance your property's security.

Strategic Placement for Maximum Security

The fundamental goal of strategic bollard placement is to create a physical and psychological barrier that deters unauthorised access or accidental damage. Start by assessing the perimeter of your property. Note the most vulnerable areas: main entrances, pedestrian pathways, and vehicle access points. These are prime locations for bollard installation.

At main entrances, bollards should be spaced closely enough to prevent vehicle penetration while allowing free movement for pedestrians and authorised vehicles. It's a delicate balance—too wide and you invite risk; too narrow and you might hinder emergency services.

For pedestrian areas, consider the visual and physical impact of bollards. You want to ensure that they are visible enough to deter vehicle intrusion without becoming an obstacle course for foot traffic. The placement should naturally guide people towards entry points without confusion.

When it comes to vehicle access points, especially for loading docks or garages, bollards must be robust enough to stop vehicles but placed in a way that does not impede business operations. Here, retractable or removable bollards can be an excellent choice, offering flexibility according to the security level needed at different times.

In each scenario, think about the type of vehicle threats you are most likely to face. Are you guarding against high-speed impacts or preventing accidental nudges from parking vehicles? This threat assessment will guide the spacing and depth of foundation for the bollards, ensuring they perform as needed in the event of an impact.

Integrating Bollards into Existing Landscapes

Integrating security features like bollards into a well-established landscape can be a challenge but think of it as an opportunity to enhance the aesthetic appeal while boosting security. The key is to design with a dual-purpose approach—security and aesthetics must go hand in hand.

Firstly, consider the existing architectural style and materials of your building and landscaping. Choose bollards that complement or accent these elements. For instance, stainless steel bollards might suit modern commercial spaces with glass and steel structures, while stone-covered bollards could blend seamlessly into more traditional settings.

Placement should also consider the natural flow of the landscape. Bollards can be used to highlight and protect garden features, artworks, or other important elements without seeming obtrusive. In areas where you expect high pedestrian traffic, consider using bollards as part of a wider traffic calming strategy. They can double as seating or display platforms for signage and lighting, merging functionality with utility.

Also, remember that the installation process might disturb existing landscapes. Plan carefully to minimise disruption. For example, if you're placing bollards near mature trees, you'll need to consider root structures and soil conditions to avoid damaging these natural assets.

Case Studies of Effective Bollard Usage

Learning from real-life contexts can provide invaluable insights into effective bollard placement. Consider these brief case studies:

1. Tech Start-Up Campus: A well-known software development company installed decorative bollards along the perimeter of its campus. The bollards were spaced to prevent car ramming attacks while featuring built-in LED lighting to enhance visibility and safety during night-time. This strategic placement not only protected the premises but also improved the campus's aesthetic and employee sense of security.

2. Historic Law Firm Office: Located in a heritage building, this law firm faced the challenge of installing security without compromising the historical façade. They opted for removable bollards that could be taken down during office hours and re-installed after hours. This strategy maintained the building's aesthetic integrity while providing flexible security.

3. Accountancy Corporation Car Park: Dealing with frequent unintentional bumps from cars in their car park, an accountancy firm implemented a combination of fixed and retractable bollards at key points. This layout managed vehicle traffic flow more effectively and reduced minor accidents, saving on repair costs over time.

By examining these examples, you can see that the strategic placement of bollards, when integrated thoughtfully into the landscape and tailored to specific needs, not only enhances security but also adds value to the property. Whether you're protecting against threats or managing traffic, the right approach to bollard placement can make all the difference in creating a secure, functional, and aesthetically pleasing environment.

Beyond Bollards: Comprehensive Perimeter Security

When you've tackled the physical barriers of bollards, your security strategy shouldn't just stop there. Enhancing your commercial property's defence goes beyond mere physical obstructions; it involves a blend of technology and environmental design. Let's dive into how you can fortify your commercial properties through electronic surveillance integration, sophisticated access control systems, and strategic landscaping.

Electronic Surveillance Integration

In the digital age, integrating electronic surveillance into your security system is paramount. This goes beyond installing a few cameras around the perimeter. Effective surveillance is about strategic placement, high-quality equipment, and integrated software solutions that keep you one step ahead of potential security breaches.

Firstly, consider the type of cameras you deploy. CCTV systems equipped with night vision and motion sensors expand your security coverage to 24/7 vigilance. Position cameras at every entrance and exit point, and consider their field of view; wide-angle lenses can help cover more ground. High-resolution cameras are crucial; they ensure that any intruder's features can be captured clearly, which is vital for identification and legal proceedings.

Moreover, modern surveillance systems offer more than just video recording. They integrate with software that provides real-time alerts to your security team or mobile device. These systems can be trained to recognise unusual activity patterns using artificial intelligence, immediately flagging any anomalies. For instance, if an individual loiters near an entrance way past business hours, your system can alert you instantly.

Remote access is another feature that enhances surveillance efficacy. It allows you or your security personnel to monitor the property from anywhere in the world, ensuring constant oversight. This is particularly beneficial if you manage multiple properties or are frequently out of town.

Access Control Systems

Your next layer of security is controlling who can enter your property and when. Access control systems range from basic keypad entry systems to advanced biometric systems, like fingerprint and facial recognition technologies. The choice of system often depends on the level of security you require, balanced against the need for ease of access for authorised personnel.

For high-value industries, biometric systems provide a robust solution as they are hard to fake or bypass. Combining this with a badge system can add an extra layer of security, ensuring double verification of identities. Moreover, modern access control systems can be integrated with other security measures. For instance, if an unauthorised attempt is made to enter a restricted area, your surveillance system can zoom in and start recording at high resolution, while security personnel are alerted immediately.

Another aspect to consider is access logging. Advanced systems maintain records of who enters and exits, and at what times, which can be crucial in the event of a security breach. It also helps in non-security situations such as payroll processing or monitoring timekeeping.

Landscaping for Security

Often overlooked, the role of landscaping in security is substantial. Thoughtful landscaping can enhance your property's defence, not just its aesthetics. Start by considering visibility; ensure that trees and shrubs are trimmed so that they do not provide cover for unauthorised individuals to hide behind. However, strategic placement of thorny plants under windows or along perimeter fences can act as a natural deterrent.

Lighting plays a crucial role in security-focused landscaping. Ensure that the property is well-lit, especially around entrances, exits, and parking areas. Motion-activated lights can be particularly effective as they surprise intruders and alert staff to movement.

Water features, while aesthetically pleasing, can also be utilised for security. For example, a strategically placed fountain near entrance points can mask conversation sounds, making it harder for eavesdroppers to listen in on private discussions.

Finally, consider the terrain of your landscape. Uneven surfaces with natural dips and elevations can be utilised to direct or limit pedestrian and vehicular access. Similarly, gravel paths can be noisy when walked on, serving as an audible alert to the presence of visitors.

Combining these elements of comprehensive perimeter security can significantly enhance the safety of your commercial property. Remember, the goal is to integrate these systems seamlessly, ensuring they work in concert to provide a full spectrum of defence, from the ground up.

RECAP AND ACTION ITEMS

Congratulations on navigating through the essentials of bollard implementation in commercial property security. You now possess a foundational understanding of bollard types, materials, and the crucial balance between aesthetics and function. Moreover, you've explored strategic placement and how to seamlessly integrate these sturdy sentinels into your property's landscape, topped off with real-world applications that showcase their effectiveness.

To move from theory to practice, here's a set of action steps designed to fortify your premises and elevate your security strategy:

1. Assess Your Current Perimeter Security: Take a walk around your property and note any potential vulnerabilities that could be mitigated with the installation of bollards. Are there areas with high pedestrian traffic that could benefit from added protection? Or perhaps vehicle access points that need to be more securely controlled?

2. Consult with a Security Architect: With your notes in hand, discuss your specific needs with a professional who can provide insight into the most effective types and placements of bollards. They can help tailor a security plan that respects both the functionality and aesthetic appeal of your property.

3. Choose the Right Materials: Reflect on the material choices for bollards discussed earlier. Consider your local climate, the level of security needed, and how these materials blend with your building's design. A well-chosen bollard can be both a visual asset and a robust barrier.

4. Plan for Integration: Think about how bollards will work in conjunction with other security measures. Will they complement your electronic surveillance systems? How will they affect the efficiency of your access control systems? Integration is key to creating a seamless security environment.

5. Implement and Review: Once your bollards are installed, don't consider it 'job done'. Regularly review their effectiveness, and be prepared to adjust your strategy based on new security challenges or changes in the use of your space.

6. Educate Your Team: Ensure that everyone from your security personnel to your front-of-house staff understands the role and function of the bollards. Proper training on the security infrastructure will enhance its effectiveness and the overall safety of your property.

By taking these steps, you will not only increase the physical security of your commercial property but also project a strong sense of safety and professionalism to your clients and visitors. Remember, security is not just about protection; it's about creating an environment where your business can thrive without fear of disruption.

4

INSIDE OUT SECURITY: SAFEGUARDING INTERIOR SPACES

"Security is not a product, but a process." – *Bruce Schneier*

Critical Areas of Focus

When protecting your commercial property, the devil is in the details—or more precisely, in the distinct areas of your building. From the bustling entry points to the hum of common areas and the confidentiality of sensitive zones, each segment demands your undivided attention. This isn't just about putting locks on doors; it's about strategic thinking and a proactive approach to safeguarding your assets and people. Let's break it down, shall we?

Entry Points

First impressions count, and in the context of building security, your entry points are the front line. They are both your welcome mat and your gatekeeper. The aim here is twofold: to facilitate smooth access for the right people and to robustly defend against unwelcome intruders.

Start by considering visibility. Are your entry points visible from the street or covered by CCTV? Obscured entrances might seem like a security measure but can actually provide cover for unauthorised activities. Clear, well-lit entryways monitored by high-definition CCTV not only deter potential security breaches but also help in identifying perpetrators should an incident occur.

Next, think about the type of barriers you employ. Traditional locks and keys are a basic necessity, but in high-stakes environments like yours, biometric systems (think fingerprint and retina scanners) can elevate your security manifold. These technologies make unauthorised access exponentially more difficult and track exactly who is coming and going, and when.

But let's not forget the human element. Security personnel play a crucial role in managing entry points. They can perform identity verifications, manage visitor access, and respond in real time to potential threats. Their presence is a powerful deterrent to opportunistic criminals.

Common Areas

Moving inward, common areas such as lobbies, cafeterias, and hallways are hubs of daily activity. These spaces are challenging to secure due to their fluid nature; they're designed to be welcoming and accessible. However, this shouldn't mean they become soft targets.

Surveillance is your best friend in these zones. Strategically placed cameras paired with live monitoring ensure that any unusual activity doesn't slip through the cracks. However, surveillance should be complemented by clear signage about security policies—these act as both information points and deterrents.

Access control within the building can significantly enhance security. Employing electronic access systems that require badges or codes to move through different sections of the building can help in containing potential breaches to isolated areas, limiting the overall vulnerability of your space.

Also, consider the layout of your common areas. Are there any obscured corners or unintentional hiding spots? A redesign might not always be feasible, but even small adjustments can enhance natural surveillance and reduce the risk of unauthorised activities.

Sensitive Internal Zones

The sanctums of your business—be it the server room of a software development company, the records room in a legal practice, or the financial documents storage in an accounting firm—require the highest level of security. Here, access must be meticulously controlled and monitored.

Physical barriers are crucial. Reinforced doors with electronic locks that record entry and exit times provide a robust first layer of defence. For an additional layer, consider installing biometric locks that require a combination of a badge and a fingerprint or iris scan to grant access.

Inside these areas, keep the principle of 'least privilege' front and centre: only those who absolutely need to enter for their work should have access. This minimises potential internal threats and simplifies monitoring.

Moreover, environmental controls such as fire suppression systems and climate controls are vital. Many sensitive materials, be they digital or paper, are vulnerable to environmental damage. Ensuring that these rooms are equipped to handle fires, floods, or other disasters is as important as guarding against theft.

In wrapping up this section, remember that securing a commercial property is a dynamic challenge. It requires a layered approach that considers the unique vulnerabilities of each area of your premises. By focusing on these critical areas—entry points, common areas, and sensitive zones—you create a robust framework for safeguarding your property. This isn't just about preventing loss; it's about creating an environment where your business can thrive safely and confidently. Remember, security is not a product but an ongoing process. Keep assessing, keep improving, and stay ahead of the risks.

Interior Reinforcement Techniques

When it comes to fortifying the interiors of your commercial properties, especially those in high-stakes industries such as software development, legal practices, and accounting, you can't be too prepared. After identifying critical areas, the next step involves beefing up your interior with robust reinforcement techniques. Let's dive into three key strategies: Safe rooms and panic rooms, reinforced interior partitions, and blast curtains and shields.

Safe Rooms and Panic Rooms

Imagine a scenario where an unexpected security breach occurs. Where do your employees go? This isn't just about having a plan; it's about having a physical space that can offer real protection when it matters most. That's where safe rooms, or panic rooms, come into play. These are secure areas within a building specifically designed to provide safety in emergencies such as armed intrusions or even natural disasters.

Designing a safe room involves several critical considerations. Firstly, the location is paramount. It should be easily accessible to all staff but not obvious or easily accessible to outsiders. Often, a central location within the building works best, as it minimises the distance anyone has to travel to reach safety.

The construction is the next vital aspect. Walls reinforced with steel or Kevlar panels can resist gunfire and physical breach attempts. For the door, you'll want something equally robust, typically made from steel, featuring multiple locks and perhaps even a biometric access system to ensure that only authorised personnel can enter.

Inside, the room should be equipped with an independent ventilation system and ideally its own power supply. Also, stock it with essentials: non-perishable foods, water, first aid supplies, and perhaps even a separate communication system that can be used if the main lines are compromised.

Reinforced Interior Partitions

Moving beyond safe rooms, another area to consider is the reinforcement of general interior spaces. Here, the use of reinforced interior partitions can significantly enhance the security of sensitive zones such as server rooms, executive offices, or any area containing valuable assets or information.

These partitions are not your average office dividers. They are constructed from high-impact materials that can withstand force and provide not only privacy but a physical barrier against intrusion. Materials range from tempered or bullet-resistant glass to solid steel panels depending on your security needs.

Furthermore, consider the acoustical properties of these partitions. In environments where sensitive information is discussed, soundproofing is just as important as physical security. Acoustic panels can be integrated to prevent eavesdropping from outside, maintaining the confidentiality of your discussions and protecting intellectual property.

Installation of these partitions also offers flexibility. Unlike permanent structural changes, many modern reinforced partitions can be relocated or reconfigured as your space needs or security strategies evolve. This adaptability makes them an excellent investment in the rapidly changing landscape of business operations and security threats.

Blast Curtains and Shields

Lastly, let's touch on an often-overlooked aspect of interior security reinforcement: blast curtains and shields. These are particularly relevant in high-risk industries or locations prone to explosive threats, whether industrial accidents or external attacks.

Blast curtains are made from high-strength, flame-resistant fabrics designed to absorb shock waves and shrapnel. They can be installed near windows or glass partitions, areas particularly vulnerable to blasts. In the event of an explosion, these curtains help prevent flying glass shards, one of the most common causes of injury in explosions.

Blast shields serve a similar purpose but are generally more rigid. These can be fixed or deployable, and they are commonly used to protect specific areas such as reception desks, check-in counters, or exposed workstations. Their implementation does not imply expecting daily threats, but it's a proactive measure to minimise risk and demonstrate to your staff and clients that their safety is taken seriously.

Implementing these interior reinforcement techniques provides not just a physical layer of security but also a psychological one. Your employees feel safer, and in turn, they perform better, knowing that their welfare is a priority. Moreover, clients and partners recognise your commitment to maintaining a secure environment, which in high-value industries, is often seen as reflective of the professionalism and reliability of your business.

Each of these techniques — from creating impenetrable safe rooms to installing blast-resistant curtains — forms a critical component of your overall security strategy. They ensure that your fortress is not just robust at the perimeter but also resilient from the inside out.

Technology Integration for Internal Security

In the realm of safeguarding your commercial property from the inside out, integrating advanced technologies is not just an option—it's a necessity. With the right systems in place, you can elevate your building's security from basic to practically impregnable. Let's dive into how technology can fortify your internal spaces, ensuring that your high-value operations are shielded against external threats.

Advanced Alarm Systems

Start by thinking about your alarm system; it's the sentinel that never sleeps. But not all alarm systems are created equal. For high-value commercial properties like yours, generic solutions just won't cut it. You need a system that's as sophisticated as the assets it's protecting.

Consider integrating biometric alarms that use fingerprint or retinal scans to control access to sensitive zones. These systems offer a level of security that is difficult to breach, and they ensure that only authorised personnel can access critical areas. Another top-tier option is seismic detectors. These can pick up any unusual vibrations within the premises—whether they're from unauthorised footsteps or the faint drilling through a wall.

Motion sensors can be customised to the layout of your building and the typical activity patterns within it. By setting up a network of smart motion detectors, you can monitor all movement in real-time. Pair these with high-definition CCTV cameras that can feed live footage to your smartphone or central security hub, and you're looking at a comprehensive surveillance package that keeps you in control, no matter where you are.

Emergency Communication Enhancements

When an incident occurs, rapid response is crucial, and this hinges on efficient communication. It's essential to have a system that not only alerts you to security breaches but also facilitates swift communication between your team and emergency services.

Start with an integrated communication system that links directly to local police, fire departments, and other emergency services. In the event of a security breach, time is of the essence, and streamlined communication can drastically reduce response times.

Enhance this system with emergency alert buttons strategically placed around sensitive zones. These should be accessible and easy to activate. Upon activation, they will send out an instant alert to the security team and, if necessary, directly to emergency responders.

Don't overlook the power of a good intercom system. Modern digital intercoms can provide clear and secure lines of communication between different parts of your building or between personnel and security teams. In a high-stress situation, being able to communicate clearly can make all the difference.

Smart Building Technologies for Security

Embracing smart building technologies can transform your property into a fortress. These systems not only improve security but also enhance the operational efficiency of the building, providing a dual benefit that's hard to ignore.

Smart locks are a great starting point. Replace traditional locks with smart locks that can be controlled remotely and customised for different levels of access. These locks can also generate user access reports, which help track who accessed which area at what time—a useful tool for post-incident analysis.

Next, consider environmental monitoring technologies. These can detect changes in air quality, temperature, or even the presence of hazardous gases. In industries like yours, where intellectual property and sensitive information are as critical as physical assets, ensuring that the environment within your building is being monitored can prevent sabotage or accidental damage.

Lastly, integrate these technologies through a centralised building management system (BMS). A BMS can monitor and control the building's security features, energy consumption, and other operational aspects from a single dashboard. This integration not only enhances security but also improves overall building efficiency, reducing costs and environmental impact.

By adopting these state-of-the-art technologies, you're not just protecting your assets; you're setting a new standard in commercial property security. Remember, in today's fast-paced and often unpredictable business environment, being proactive about security isn't just a strategy—it's a necessity. With these tools at your disposal, you can rest assured that your premises are well-protected, allowing you to focus on growing your business securely and with peace of mind.

RECAP AND ACTION ITEMS

You've just navigated through the essentials of tightening security from the inside out of your commercial properties. By focusing on critical areas such as entry points, common areas, and sensitive internal zones, you're already stepping up your game against potential threats. But remember, recognising these areas is just the starting line.

The journey towards a fortress-like security doesn't end at identification; it thrives on reinforcement. Incorporating safe rooms, reinforced interior partitions, and blast curtains can drastically enhance your building's resilience against extreme situations. These aren't merely upgrades; they are investments in peace of mind and the continuity of your business.

Advancing further, the integration of cutting-edge technology like advanced alarm systems, emergency communication enhancements, and smart building technologies not only fortifies security but also ensures that it is seamlessly woven into the fabric of your daily operations. These systems provide a robust framework that can alert you to issues in real-time, helping you to respond swiftly and effectively.

Now, what's next? Here are some action steps to consider:

1. Assess and Audit: Walk through your property with a security professional to identify vulnerable spots and evaluate the effectiveness of existing security measures.

2. Plan Upgrades: Based on your assessment, prioritise which security enhancements are most critical. Start with the most vulnerable areas and plan a phased upgrade, integrating more robust security features over time.

3. Technology Consultation: Consult with a tech expert specialising in security systems for businesses like yours. Discuss smart technologies that can be integrated into your existing systems for a smoother transition.

4. Staff Training: Organise regular training sessions for your staff to familiarise them with new security protocols and technologies. Ensure they understand how to act during different types of emergencies.

5. Review and Revise: Security is an ongoing process. Regularly review and update your security measures to adapt to new threats and incorporate technological advances.

By taking these steps, you not only safeguard your assets and personnel but also fortify the reputation of your business as a secure and resilient operation. Remember, in high-stakes industries, the strength of your internal security can be as crucial as the quality of the services you provide.

5

THE HUMAN FACTOR: TRAINING AND PREPAREDNESS

"Security is the chief enemy of mortals." - William Shakespeare

Creating a Security Culture

In the bustling ecosystem of high-value industries—where your enterprise, be it in software development, legal practice, or accounting, not only flourishes but also becomes a potential target—security transcends beyond mere necessity; it evolves into a pivotal component of your operational ethos. Cultivating a security culture within your organisation is less about installing the most expensive alarms and more about weaving awareness, preparedness, and responsiveness into the very fabric of your company. Let's delve into how you can architect a robust security culture that not only protects but also empowers your team and business.

Training Programs for Staff

Initiating a transformation in workplace culture begins with comprehensive training programs. These programs serve as the bedrock upon which vigilant and responsive behaviours are built. For commercial building owners, particularly in sectors laden with sensitive information or expensive assets, staff training isn't just about going through the motions—it's about creating a proactive security mindset.

Start by identifying the specific risks associated with your industry. Does your software development firm need to guard against cyber-attacks? Does your legal practice handle sensitive client information that could be a target for corporate espionage? Tailor your training sessions to address these unique challenges, ensuring they are relevant and engaging. It's crucial that training isn't seen as a one-off or annual chore but as an ongoing process that keeps pace with evolving threats.

Incorporate interactive modules, such as role-playing scenarios that involve handling potential security breaches or recognising phishing attempts. These practical exercises are far more effective than purely theoretical lessons. Moreover, invite security experts who can share real-world experiences and solutions that resonate with your staff, making the threats and their implications more tangible.

Encourage feedback during these sessions. This not only helps you gauge the effectiveness of your training but also promotes a culture where security is openly discussed, not whispered about in corridors or ignored.

Encouraging Vigilance and Awareness

Vigilance is the cornerstone of a security culture. It's about maintaining a constant state of awareness and being able to recognise and report suspicious activities. This can only happen in an environment where every member of the team feels responsible for the collective security.

Communicate clearly that security is part of everyone's job description. You can foster this mindset by integrating security-related metrics into performance reviews. Recognise and reward behaviours that enhance the firm's security. Simple acknowledgements or incentives for employees who consistently follow security protocols or who have identified potential threats can make a significant difference.

Moreover, use signage and reminders throughout your property to reinforce the importance of vigilance. Whether it's a reminder to lock computers when they are not in use or prompts to report unrecognized individuals in private areas, these small cues can help in maintaining high levels of alertness.

Handling Security Breaches

Despite the best preventive measures, the possibility of a security breach cannot be entirely ruled out. How your organisation responds to such an incident can either mitigate or exacerbate the situation. Thus, preparing your staff for this possibility is essential.

First, develop a clear, structured plan on how to handle various types of security breaches—be it data theft, a physical break-in, or a cyber-attack. Ensure that all employees know whom to contact immediately when they suspect a breach. This could be a designated security officer or an external cybersecurity team.

Training should also cover the importance of containment and control. Employees should know the basic do's and don'ts during a breach. For instance, in the case of a cyber-attack, the instinct might be to shut down systems or delete suspicious files, which could potentially destroy valuable evidence. Instead, staff should be trained to isolate affected systems and await further instructions from the IT security team.

Regular drills that simulate different breach scenarios can also be invaluable. These exercises not only test the responsiveness of your team but also highlight any weaknesses in your current protocols, providing crucial insights for improvement.

By addressing these three critical areas—tailored training programs, fostering vigilance, and effective breach management—you lay the groundwork for a security culture that not only anticipates threats but also enhances the overall resilience of your business. Remember, in high-stakes industries, a well-prepared team is your best defence.

Emergency Response Planning

When the sirens sound or disaster strikes, your response in the initial moments can significantly sway the outcome, not just for your property but, more crucially, for the safety of your team. Let's dive into the essentials of crafting a robust emergency response plan that safeguards not only your assets but, importantly, your people.

Evacuation Procedures

Imagine the fire alarm goes off on a busy afternoon. What happens next in your building can either be orderly or chaotic, and the difference lies in your preparedness. Here's how you can ensure it's the former:

1. Clear Signage and Information: Start by ensuring that evacuation routes are clearly marked and well known to all employees. Regular walkthroughs and drills can help make these routes second nature. Remember, in an emergency, confusion is your biggest enemy.

2. Role Assignments: Assign specific roles to staff members.

You need floor wardens who'll ensure everyone leaves their area, and you might consider special assistants for individuals with disabilities. These roles should be assigned ahead of time and integrated into regular training sessions.

3. Regular Drills: Conducting regular evacuation drills is like the rehearsal before the big show. It ensures everyone knows their part and can perform it even under pressure. You might find it a hassle, but the reality is simple: practice makes perfect, and perfect could save lives.

4. Feedback and Improvement: After each drill, gather feedback. What went well? What could go smoother? Use this information to tweak and improve your procedures. This isn't just about compliance; it's about continuous improvement.

First Aid and Trauma Readiness

When accidents happen, the immediate response can dramatically affect outcomes. Here's how to ensure you're ready to handle injuries until professional help arrives:

1. Adequate Training: First aid training isn't just for your designated health and safety officer. In high-risk environments, or simply to enhance your team's confidence, consider training multiple team members in first aid and CPR.

2. Accessible First Aid Kits: Your building should have multiple, well-stocked first aid kits. These should be accessible and their locations should be known to all employees. Regular checks to ensure they are fully stocked and that nothing has expired are essential.

3. Trauma Kits for High-Risk Areas: If your business involves higher risks, standard first aid might not suffice. Consider equipping your premises with trauma kits which include items like tourniquets and haemostatic agents. Training on how to use these items is crucial and can be a lifesaver while waiting for emergency services.

4. Mental Health First Aid: Often overlooked, psychological first aid is vital, especially after traumatic events. Training in mental health support can help your team manage stress and trauma, supporting both immediate and long-term recovery.

Coordination with Local Law Enforcement

In events like break-ins or active threats, your relationship with local law enforcement can significantly impact the speed and effectiveness of their response. Here's how to ensure this relationship is solid:

1. Pre-incident Planning: Invite local police to visit your premises. They can offer invaluable advice on security improvements and emergency response. This also lets them familiarise themselves with your layout, which can be crucial in an emergency.

2. Contact Information: Ensure you have up-to-date contact information for your local police station, and they have yours. This includes after-hours contacts. In crisis situations, time is of the essence, and fumbling for phone numbers is the last thing you want.

3. Joint Drills and Simulations: If possible, organise joint emergency drills with local law enforcement. This not only tests your plans but also builds a rapport with the officers who will respond to calls from your property.

4. Shared Intelligence: If there's a known threat in your area, whether it's a spate of break-ins or cyber threats, sharing this information with local police can help them better protect your locality. Similarly, they can provide you with intelligence that could prevent an incident at your premises.

By integrating these elements into your emergency response planning, you create a framework that not only responds efficiently to immediate threats but also builds a foundation of safety and security that permeates your company culture. Remember, in the world of high stakes and high value, being prepared isn't just an option; it's a necessity.

Continuity Planning for Business Operations

In the unpredictable whirlwind of running a high-value commercial business, crises are not a matter of if, but when. Your ability to bounce back hinges significantly on the robustness of your continuity plans. This isn't just about surviving the initial blow; it's about ensuring your operations thrive and continue seamlessly, keeping your enterprise resilient in the face of adversity.

Data and IT Security in Crises

In today's digital age, your data is your most valuable asset, especially in sectors like legal practices, software development, and accountancy. Protecting this data during a crisis ensures that the core functions of your business can continue without a hitch. The first step is to understand the potential threats to your IT infrastructure. These can range from cyberattacks and data breaches to natural disasters that physically damage your hardware.

Implementing robust encryption is a foundational step. Encryption acts like an unbreachable lock on your data, ensuring that even if data is stolen, it remains unreadable to the thief. Regular updates to your software and systems also close any vulnerabilities that could be exploited by new strains of malware or hacking tactics.

However, the real game-changer is the adoption of cloud-based services. By storing your data offsite, you not only protect it from physical damage but also ensure it can be accessed remotely by your team, regardless of their location. This flexibility is crucial in maintaining business operations even when your physical office is compromised.

Moreover, regularly scheduled backups, both on physical drives and in the cloud, are your safety net. Should you lose access to your primary data sources, these backups serve as a fail-safe, enabling a swift restoration of data and minimal disruption to your services.

Backup and Recovery Strategies

Now, let's talk recovery. It's all well and good to back up your data, but if your recovery process is as slow as a snail, it's little comfort. You need a strategy that is not only robust but rapid.

Start by defining your Recovery Time Objectives (RTO) and Recovery Point Objectives (RPO). RTO is how quickly you need to recover your IT and data services to avoid unacceptable consequences associated with a break in business continuity. RPO, on the other hand, determines the maximum age of files that must be recovered from backup storage for normal operations to resume without causing any significant data loss.

The next step is to automate your backup processes. Automation reduces the risk of human error and ensures that backups are done consistently and on schedule. Consider using real-time replication for your most critical data; this method continuously captures changes to data almost simultaneously. In the event of a system failure, you can switch to a backup server that holds a near-current copy of your data, reducing downtime drastically.

Testing your backup systems regularly cannot be overstated.

It's like a fire drill for your data. These tests will reveal any flaws in your recovery plan, giving you a chance to rectify them before an actual crisis occurs. Remember, a backup is only as good as its ability to be restored.

Keeping Business Operational Post-Incident

After ensuring that your data can survive a crisis, your next focus should be on maintaining operational continuity. This encompasses more than just technological readiness; it involves strategic planning and employee readiness to adapt to temporary working conditions.

One effective strategy is to develop a tiered response plan that prioritises services that are critical to your operations. Not all business functions are created equal, and recognising this will help you allocate resources more effectively during a crisis.

Remote work capabilities are now a cornerstone of operational continuity. The recent global shift towards remote working environments has demonstrated that many jobs can be done effectively from home. Ensuring your staff has the necessary tools and resources to work remotely is not just about crisis management; it's about adapting to the modern work landscape.

Communication is your glue in times of crisis. Establish clear communication channels and protocols with your employees, clients, and stakeholders. In the heat of a crisis, miscommunication can escalate the situation. Regular updates through emails, instant messaging, and virtual meetings can help maintain clarity and continuity.

Lastly, engage with continuity experts or consultants who can provide an external perspective on your plans. These professionals can offer insights that internal teams might overlook and help you craft a continuity strategy that is comprehensive and tailored to the specific needs of your industry.

By integrating these strategies into your business continuity planning, you're not just preparing to survive; you're setting up your business to thrive and prosper, irrespective of the challenges that may come your way. Remember, the goal is to make your business as resilient as possible, turning potential disasters into mere hiccups on your path to success.

RECAP AND ACTION ITEMS

Congratulations on powering through the essentials of fortifying your commercial estate against the unpredictable. You've now laid the groundwork for a robust security culture, developed a keen sense of emergency response preparedness, and strategised for maintaining business continuity—imperative gears in the machine of a thriving, resilient business.

1. Implement Your Security Culture Training: Kick off by scheduling the first round of security training sessions for your team. Make these engaging and informative. Remember, the goal is to embed a culture of awareness and vigilance, not just check a box. Consider role-playing exercises that simulate potential security breaches to make the learning experience visceral.

2. Drill Your Emergency Procedures: Time to get practical. Organise quarterly drills to go over evacuation procedures and first aid response. These drills should involve everyone in your building, from the top executives to the newest hires. Include scenarios that are likely given your geographic location and business type—this isn't just about fires and earthquakes but also about potential threats specific to high-value industries, like data breaches or intellectual property theft.

3. Sync with Local Law Enforcement: Reach out to your local police department to discuss your security plans and how they can offer support or advice. This collaboration can be invaluable, especially in creating response strategies that are swift and effective. Law enforcement agencies may also provide additional training or insights specific to threats in your area.

4. Audit Your IT Security Measures: Given that much of your operation is likely reliant on digital processes, ensure your IT security is ironclad. Regularly update your systems, conduct penetration testing, and review access controls. Keep your team informed about the latest in cyber security threats and how to counteract them.

5. Review Your Backup Strategies: Regularly test your data backup systems to ensure they work when needed. This isn't a set-it-and-forget-it type deal. Your backup and recovery protocols should evolve as new technologies and threats emerge.

6. Plan for the Unexpected: Finally, always keep an eye on the horizon. The business landscape, especially in high-stakes industries, changes rapidly. Regular reviews and updates to your preparedness plans will keep you nimble and ready to pivot as challenges arise.

By embedding these practices into your business routine, you safeguard not just your physical assets but the continuity of your services, the welfare of your employees, and the trust of your clients. Remember, a well-prepared business is not only a secure business but also a competitive and resilient one. Let's get to work!

6

ASSESSING THREATS: UNDERSTANDING RISK

"Uncertainty and expectation are the joys of life. Security is an insipid thing." - William Congreve

Types of Threats and Their Origins

When you're in the business of protecting your commercial property, understanding the landscape of potential threats is crucial. The world isn't just evolving technologically; the nature of threats to high-value industries like yours—be it software game development, legal practice, or accountancy—is also shifting. Let's dive into the murky waters of threats and their origins, so you can better shield your assets and ensure your fortress remains unbreachable.

Terrorism

The word itself can send shivers down the spine. Terrorism isn't confined to dramatic acts on government buildings or public spaces; it has insidiously woven its way into more targeted areas, including commercial sectors that hold high-value data or intellectual property. For businesses like yours, the risk isn't necessarily about the common portrayal of terrorism; it's more about the lesser-known, yet potentially devastating, cyberterrorism threats.

Imagine your latest game development project or your clients' sensitive legal documents falling into the hands of a terrorist group aiming to manipulate stock prices, influence legal outcomes, or sway public opinion by threatening data exposure. The motives might range from political to financial, often blurring the lines between mere cybercrime and terrorism.

To understand and combat this, you need to peel back the layers of who might benefit from destabilizing your industry. Is it a rival state? A radical group looking to make a statement? Or competitors hiding in the shadows? Often, the origins are complex, tied to global tensions and facilitated by local vulnerabilities in your cybersecurity armour.

Corporate Espionage

Now, let's talk about a more 'cloak and dagger' kind of threat—corporate espionage. It's not just for the movies. In a world where a single piece of code or a client list can be worth millions, knowing who might have their eyes on your proprietary data is essential.

Corporate spies can come from anywhere—rival companies, disgruntled employees, or professional espionage contractors. They're often driven by the potential for significant financial gain or strategic advantage. The methods used can range from sophisticated hacking tools, social engineering tactics, to internal data theft. The origins of such threats are frequently linked to competitive pressures within the industry. The higher the stakes, the more tempting the target.

For someone managing a software development company, the threat might be a competitor eager to leapfrog your latest innovation. For a legal firm, it could be about getting a sneak peek at argument strategies or client information. Understanding these motivations will guide you in crafting defences that are as much about psychology and strategy as they are about technology.

Domestic Threats

While the spectre of international intrigue and corporate sabotage looms large, sometimes the threat originates much closer to home. Domestic threats often stem from within the organisation or from local criminals who see an opportunity. These can be the most challenging to predict and prevent because they exploit familiarity and access.

Internal threats might include employees who feel slighted or see an opportunity to profit through data theft or sabotage. External domestic threats could look like burglaries, vandalism, or local hackers trying their luck. The origins here are often opportunistic, driven by proximity and ease of access to your commercial property or digital networks.

For instance, an employee in your gaming company might upload game designs to a competitor or a cloud server they control, not out of malice but for a misguided sense of securing their own future in the industry. Or perhaps a local criminal gang targets your accounting firm's physical servers, mistaking them for easy pickings.

Navigating through the quagmire of potential threats to your commercial property involves not just recognising these threats but understanding their roots. Each type of threat—be it as faceless as terrorism, as sneaky as corporate espionage, or as familiar as domestic risks—carries its own set of origins, motives, and implications. By dissecting these, you're better positioned to fortify your business against the myriad dangers lurking in today's globalised, interconnected world. As you move forward, keep these insights in mind when assessing your property's vulnerabilities and crafting a robust defence strategy.

Risk Assessment Methodologies

Quantitative vs. Qualitative Approaches

As you navigate the complex world of risk management, diving into the methodologies used for risk assessment is akin to choosing between a surgeon's scalpel and a painter's brush. Both quantitative and qualitative approaches offer unique benefits and, depending on your specific scenario, one might suit you better than the other—or perhaps a blend of both.

Starting with the quantitative realm, this approach is all about numbers. Think of it as the surgeon's scalpel—precise, measurable, and data-driven. Here, you'll employ statistical tools to forecast probabilities and potential impacts of identified risks. This method is particularly useful when you need to convince stakeholders or insurers with hard facts. For example, using past burglary data in your area, you can calculate the likelihood of this threat to your legal practice or software development firm, determining potential financial losses.

On the flip side, you've got the qualitative approach, which is more subjective but incredibly valuable. Picture this as the painter's brush—broad, nuanced, and somewhat interpretive. This method involves assessing risks based on scenarios and informed opinions, often drawing from the expertise of seasoned professionals. For instance, you might evaluate the risk of corporate espionage by discussing with a security expert who understands the subtle signs and potential threats specific to high-stakes industries like yours.

For you, the best approach often lies in merging these two. Use quantitative data to get the clear numbers and qualitative insights for those grey areas that numbers can't fully explain. This hybrid strategy can provide a comprehensive outlook on potential risks, making your decision-making process both informed and adaptable.

Tools and Technologies for Risk Assessment

Stepping up your game in risk management involves not just keen intuition but also leveraging the right tools and technologies. In today's digital age, there's a plethora of options designed to streamline and enhance the risk assessment process. Let's unpack some of the essentials that could be game-changers for your business.

Firstly, consider risk assessment software. These platforms are designed to handle large data sets and complex algorithms that help predict and quantify risks. They can be particularly useful for carrying out those quantitative analyses we talked about. For example, software like Risk Management Studio or LogicManager isn't just about crunching numbers; they also help in creating risk matrices and dashboards that give you a bird's-eye view of where your vulnerabilities might lie.

Then there's the integration of AI and machine learning, which can take your risk assessment capabilities to another level.

These technologies are adept at identifying patterns that the human eye might miss. Imagine an AI tool that scans through transaction records to flag unusual activities that could indicate fraud or breaches—essential for accountancy firms or legal practices dealing with sensitive client data.

Don't overlook the power of surveillance technologies, either. Advanced CCTV systems with motion detectors, or access control systems that use biometrics, can significantly deter physical threats to your property. The data collected from these tools can be analysed to understand traffic patterns and identify suspicious activities, thus feeding into both your qualitative and quantitative assessments.

Vulnerability Analysis

Once you've got a handle on the types of risks and the tools at your disposal, it's time to drill down into vulnerability analysis. This is where you identify the chinks in your armour—be it in your physical infrastructure, your digital defences, or even in human elements.

Begin by looking at your physical premises. For a software game developer, this might mean assessing the security of servers where your games and user data are stored. Are there adequate firewalls? Is the physical access to these servers tightly controlled? Similarly, for a law firm, the focus might be on secure document storage capabilities. Are your filing systems lockable and fireproof? Is sensitive information encrypted?

Moving to digital vulnerabilities, cybersecurity is a must-consider area. Employ penetration testing to simulate an attack on your systems and identify weaknesses before real hackers do. Also, consider the human element—often the weakest link in the security chain. Regular training sessions on security best practices can mitigate risks that stem from human error or oversight.

Each step in vulnerability analysis should lead to actionable insights. It's not just about identifying vulnerabilities but also understanding how they could be exploited and the potential impact on your business. This clarity is crucial in prioritising mitigation strategies, ensuring that you're not just fighting fires, but preventing them wherever possible.

Through careful consideration of these methodologies, tools, and analytical techniques, you can construct a robust framework for understanding and managing the risks associated with your high-value commercial property. Remember, in the realm of risk assessment, knowledge is not just power—it's also protection.

Implementing a Risk Management Plan

Prioritising Risks

Let's jump right in. Picture your commercial property like a complex, intricate puzzle. Each piece represents a potential risk, and not all pieces are created equal. The art of prioritising risks is about identifying which pieces, if misplaced or lost, would prevent the puzzle from being completed.

How do you start? First, remember that not all risks are equally likely, and not all have the same potential impact. It's about balancing the probability of an event occurring against the severity of its consequences if it does. Start with a simple list of all identified risks from your earlier assessment. Now, rank these risks based on their potential impact and the likelihood of them occurring. Tools like risk matrices can be handy here, allowing you to visually plot risks on a chart, helping clarify which ones need immediate attention.

For instance, if you run a software development company housed in a bustling city centre, a high-impact risk could be cyber-attacks, which are also increasingly likely. On the other hand, something like an earthquake might be devastating but far less probable if you're not in a prone area.

Once you've mapped out your risks, it's crucial to focus on the ones that sit in the 'high probability, high impact' quadrant of your matrix. These are your top priorities. It doesn't mean you ignore the less critical risks, but you allocate resources and attention proportionately to ensure you're covering the most threatening bases first.

Mitigation Strategies

With your priorities set, it's time to build your fortress – metaphorically speaking. Mitigation strategies are the defences you deploy to reduce the likelihood of risks occurring and to lessen their impact if they do occur.

Each identified high-priority risk will require a tailored strategy depending on the nature of the risk and your specific business environment. Let's talk about a few general approaches:

1. Prevention: This is about taking actions to prevent a risk from occurring. For instance, if data theft is a significant concern for your legal practice, implementing robust cybersecurity measures such as firewalls, encryption, and secure authentication protocols becomes crucial.

2. Reduction: Sometimes, completely preventing a risk isn't feasible. In this case, you look to reduce either the likelihood of the risk occurring or the impact if it does. Continuing with the cybersecurity example, regular security audits and updating your systems can reduce the likelihood of a successful cyber attack.

3. Transference: This involves shifting the risk to a third party, typically through insurance or outsourcing. For game developers, this might mean using cloud servers maintained by a reputable provider to mitigate data loss risks.

4. Acceptance: Sometimes, the cost of mitigating a risk may outweigh the potential loss. In such cases, you might choose to accept the risk. This decision should be informed and strategic, not resigned. For instance, a small accounting firm may decide that the cost of top-tier cybersecurity measures is too prohibitive compared to the risk of a breach.

Implementing these strategies requires a mix of tactical actions and strategic thinking. Always ask yourself: Does this strategy align with my overall business objectives? Is it cost-effective? How does it fit with other risk mitigation strategies?

Regular Review and Updates

The only constant is change, especially in high-value, dynamic industries like yours. Hence, a risk management plan is not a one-time setup but a living process that needs regular reviews and updates.

Why is this crucial? Because both internal and external conditions change. New technologies emerge, legal requirements evolve, your business grows, and so do its assets and value. Each of these factors can alter your risk profile.

Here's how you can keep your risk management plan fresh and relevant:

1. Schedule Regular Reviews: Depending on your business's nature and the environment you operate in, set a regular schedule for reviewing your risk management plan. For high-risk environments, this could be as often as every quarter. For others, annually might suffice.

2. Stay Informed: Keep abreast of changes in your industry, as well as broader changes like new laws or technologies that could affect your risk landscape. Subscribing to industry newsletters, attending webinars, and participating in relevant forums can be beneficial.

3. Engage Your Team: Your employees often have insights into potential risks and vulnerabilities that you might not see. Regularly engaging with your team to discuss these issues can be incredibly valuable. Consider establishing a routine where team members can report concerns or suggestions related to risks.

4. Test Your Strategies: It's one thing to plan; it's another to know your plans work. Conduct simulations or drills, especially for critical areas like emergency response or IT security. These tests can reveal unforeseen flaws or areas for improvement in your strategies.

5. Document Everything: Keep detailed records of your risk assessments, mitigation actions, review dates, and changes made over time. This documentation will not only help you track your progress but will also be invaluable during audits or inspections and when onboarding new team members.

By turning these practices into routine, you ensure that your risk management plan remains a robust, dynamic tool that protects and enhances the value of your commercial property.

Remember, in the world of high-stakes commercial property management, being proactive about risk is not just wise—it's essential.

RECAP AND ACTION ITEMS

You've just armed yourself with a robust understanding of the risks that your commercial property might face—from the unnerving threats of terrorism and corporate espionage to the more commonplace but equally disruptive domestic threats. Knowledge is power, but it's only the starting point. Let's roll up our sleeves and dive into what you can do next to transform this knowledge into a fortress of security for your valuable asset.

Firstly, revisit the various threats and their origins you've explored. Take a moment to reflect on which of these threats are most likely to impact your specific business environment. Are you in a bustling city centre where the spectre of terrorism might loom larger, or is the quiet undercut by the risk of domestic upheaval or espionage sparked by local competition?

Moving on, you've delved into both quantitative and qualitative approaches to risk assessment. Now, it's time to pick the tools and technologies that align best with your business needs and budget. Whether you opt for sophisticated software that quantifies risk probabilities or qualitative assessments that provide deeper insight into less tangible threats, ensure these tools are integrated seamlessly into your daily operations.

With your risk assessment tools selected, conduct a thorough vulnerability analysis. This isn't a one-off job; make it a part of your routine. Regularly update this analysis to reflect new threats or changes in your business model. The landscape of risk is never static, and neither should your approach to managing it.

Next, prioritise the risks you've identified. Not all threats are created equal, and your resources aren't infinite. Focus on the risks that could have the most severe impact on your business. Develop mitigation strategies for these top-tier risks. This might mean anything from enhancing physical security and cyber defences to training your staff in security best practices.

Finally, remember that risk management is a dynamic process. Schedule regular reviews of your risk management plan. The effectiveness of any plan lies in its ability to adapt and evolve. As you implement changes, monitor their impact and be prepared to tweak your strategies accordingly.

In summary, you've equipped yourself with the tools and strategies to not just protect but also to prosper. Take these insights, tailor them to your unique situation, and fortify your commercial property against the threats of today and tomorrow. Take action today, and sleep better tonight knowing you're on top of the game.

7

LEGAL AND COMPLIANCE CONSIDERATIONS

"Injustice anywhere is a threat to justice everywhere." - Martin Luther King Jr.

Building Regulations and Standards

Navigating the labyrinth of building regulations and standards is akin to playing a strategic game where the rules must be meticulously followed to ensure victory. As a commercial property owner in high-value industries such as software game development, legal practices, or accounting, you face unique challenges that demand a keen understanding of local and national security regulations, compliance with fire safety and accessibility, and consideration of environmental impacts. Let's break down these critical areas to help you not only comply but thrive in creating a secure, accessible, and environmentally responsible commercial property.

Local and National Security Regulations

In the realm of commercial property ownership, understanding and adhering to security regulations is paramount. These regulations are not just bureaucratic checkboxes but are designed to protect your assets, intellectual property, and the people who move through your spaces every day.

Starting locally, you'll find that security requirements can vary significantly from one municipality to another. It's essential to engage with local building authorities or a consultant who specialises in local code compliance. Whether it's the installation of surveillance systems, controlled access points, or other security measures, local statutes could dictate not only the types of equipment you can use but also how and where they can be installed.

On a national level, particularly in high-value industries like yours, there may be additional standards to meet, often influenced by national security concerns or industry-specific regulations. For example, if you're housing a software development company with access to sensitive governmental contracts, the level of security mandated by national law could be significantly higher. Compliance here could involve anything from biometric access controls to advanced cyber-security measures.

Staying abreast of these regulations requires a proactive approach. Regularly review updates from relevant legal bodies and perhaps consider subscribing to a service that alerts you to regulatory changes. Remember, non-compliance can lead to hefty fines or, worse, a devastating breach of security that could tarnish your reputation and financial stability.

Complying with Fire Safety and Accessibility

Fire safety is a non-negotiable aspect of building management that intertwines closely with accessibility. These elements ensure a safe environment for all occupants and can significantly affect the insurance premiums and liability coverage of your property.

Fire safety compliance starts with the basics such as properly maintained and accessible fire exits, fire alarms, sprinkler systems, and extinguishers. However, for commercial properties, especially those in high-value sectors, the requirements can be more stringent. Regular audits by fire safety officers can help you stay compliant and ensure that all your fire safety equipment meets the current standards.

Accessibility, meanwhile, is about ensuring equal access to all potential users of your building. This includes adequate wheelchair access, user-friendly elevator systems, and visually accessible signage. The Equality Act 2010 provides a comprehensive framework for accessibility requirements in the UK. In the US the Americans with Disabilities Act (ADA) of 1990, ensures your building is accessible is not only a legal mandate but also a moral one, reflecting your business's values of inclusivity and respect for all individuals.

Combining fire safety and accessibility might seem daunting, but many measures serve both purposes. For instance, clear, unobstructed pathways can aid both in quick evacuations during a fire and easier movement for people with disabilities. Regular training for your staff on both fronts can also help in maintaining these standards effortlessly.

Environmental Impact Considerations

Today's commercial property owner has to think beyond the immediate confines of their buildings. The environmental impact of your property is now a significant aspect of your operational responsibility. Sustainable practices are not just good for the planet; they resonate well with customers, employees, and stakeholders, particularly in high-value, high-visibility sectors.

Start with energy efficiency – a key area where environmental impact can be mitigated. This includes everything from using energy-efficient lighting and HVAC systems to exploring renewable energy sources like solar panels. Not only do these efforts reduce your carbon footprint, but they can also lead to significant cost savings over time.

Water conservation is another critical area. Employing low-flow fixtures and sustainable water management systems can dramatically reduce your property's water usage. Additionally, consider the materials used in the construction or renovation of your building. Opting for sustainable, locally-sourced materials can reduce environmental impact and often comes with the added benefit of enhancing your building's aesthetic appeal.

Lastly, waste management should be a priority. Implementing comprehensive recycling programs and reducing waste can not only minimise your environmental impact but also comply with local regulations that increasingly mandate such practices.

Navigating these regulatory waters is not merely about compliance but about setting a standard in your industry for safety, accessibility, and environmental stewardship. As you fortify your commercial property against various risks, you also build a fortress of trust and reliability around your business.

Insurance and Liability

Navigating the labyrinth of insurance requirements for high-risk businesses can often feel like decoding a particularly cryptic piece of ancient scripture. As the owner of a commercial property in industries such as software development, legal services, or accounting, the stakes are exceptionally high, given the sensitive data and valuable assets typically involved. Consequently, ensuring that you have robust insurance coverage isn't just advisable; it's a critical component of your risk management strategy.

Insurance Requirements for High-Risk Businesses

Each industry will have its specific set of risks. For instance, software game developers might face risks related to intellectual property theft or data breaches, while legal practices must consider the implications of confidentiality breaches or loss of client-sensitive information. Similarly, accountants deal with huge volumes of personal financial data that can be catastrophic if mishandled or accessed unlawfully. For businesses like these, standard commercial property insurance might not suffice. You'll need to delve into specialised policies that address the unique risks your industry bears.

Start by understanding the basic coverage areas: property insurance, liability insurance, business interruption insurance, and cyber liability insurance are fundamental. However, the devil is in the detail. Engage with insurance brokers who are well-versed in your industry's specific challenges. They can tailor policies that cover gaps which generic policies might overlook. For example, if your business is software development, your broker might recommend a technology errors and omissions policy alongside a cyber liability policy, providing coverage against software failures or data breaches that could lead to significant financial losses for your clients.

Moreover, in high-value industries, the cost of an insurance premium is far outweighed by the potential cost of an uncovered incident. Consider it this way: if a data breach were to occur and sensitive client information were stolen from your legal practice, the fallout could include hefty fines, legal fees, and severe damage to your reputation. Insurance that covers data breaches and provides for public relations management in the aftermath can be a lifesaver in such scenarios.

Managing Liability Through Design

Moving on to Managing liability through design, it's clear that the layout and design of your building can significantly impact your legal liabilities. Thoughtful design that prioritises security and safety can mitigate risks, potentially lowering insurance premiums and certainly reducing the likelihood of costly lawsuits.

For instance, consider accessibility. Ensuring that your property is accessible not only complies with regulations like the Equality Act 2010 or US ADA Act 1990 but also reduces the risk of discrimination lawsuits. Simple measures such as adequate signage, accessible entry points, and user-friendly security protocols all contribute to a safer environment for visitors and employees alike.

Fire safety is another crucial area. Compliance with regulatory requirements is mandatory, but going beyond the minimum requirements can further protect your investments. Integrated smoke alarms, well-marked and unobstructed fire exits, and regular safety drills contribute to a safer workplace while actively demonstrating your commitment to stakeholder safety.

Surveillance systems and secure data storage locations can also play a significant role in design considerations. However, these must be balanced with privacy laws and ethical considerations, which brings us to the importance of transparency and community relations, which will be discussed later.

Case law and Precedent

Lastly, let's explore Case law and precedent. Understanding previous legal cases in your industry can provide invaluable insights into potential pitfalls and areas where your property's liability could be tested. For example, a landmark case could have been decided on the basis that a firm failed to adequately secure client data against cyber-attacks, leading to a substantial legal settlement.

Staying informed about such precedents can guide you in fortifying your own practices against similar vulnerabilities. Regular consultations with legal experts specialising in commercial property and your specific industry can keep you updated on new and relevant case law. This proactive approach not only helps in managing risks but also aids in shaping policies and procedures that align with legal expectations and industry standards.

By adopting comprehensive insurance solutions tailored to your specific business needs, integrating thoughtful design to manage liability, and keeping abreast of relevant legal precedents, you fortify your commercial property against potential threats. These strategies not only protect your physical assets but also safeguard your business reputation, ensuring that you continue to thrive in a competitive, high-stakes environment. Remember, in the realm of high-value industries, being proactive about insurance and liability isn't just good practice—it's essential for your business's longevity and success.

Ethics and Privacy Concerns

In the labyrinth of securing your commercial property, the intersection of ethics and privacy rights often resembles a tightrope walk. It's about finding that sweet spot where security measures respect individual privacy while safeguarding the assets and intellectual property that fuel your business. As you navigate this delicate balance, several key considerations come into play.

Balancing Security with Privacy Rights

First and foremost, it's crucial to establish a security strategy that does not infringe on the privacy rights of your employees, clients, and visitors. In today's digital age, surveillance technologies such as CCTV cameras and biometric systems are commonplace in commercial properties. However, their use raises significant privacy concerns that must be addressed thoughtfully.

To start, you should ensure transparency in your surveillance practices. This means clearly communicating to all stakeholders the type and scope of surveillance being conducted. For instance, placing visible signs that notify the presence of CCTV cameras can demystify surveillance and reduce feelings of intrusion.

Moreover, consider the placement of these cameras. Areas such as restrooms or changing rooms are off-limits, as surveillance in these locations can lead to severe privacy violations and legal repercussions. Instead, focus on installing cameras in public spaces where security concerns are more prevalent, such as lobbies, parking lots, and around perimeter fences.

Another aspect to consider is data protection. The data collected via surveillance must be handled according to the principles set out in the UK's Data Protection Act 2018, which encompasses the General Data Protection Regulation (GDPR). The US Stored Communications Act (SCA) is very similar and ensures that any personal data captured – be it video footage or access logs – must be stored securely, used responsibly, and retained only for as long as necessary. You should also be prepared to provide individuals access to their data if requested and delete it when it's no longer needed for the purpose it was collected.

Ethical Considerations in Surveillance

While the legal framework provides a baseline, ethical surveillance practices can elevate your reputation and ensure a harmonious workplace. It's about going beyond what's legal to what's morally sound. For instance, consider implementing a policy where employees have a say in the surveillance methods applied in their workspaces. This inclusion can alleviate concerns and foster a culture of trust and respect.

Furthermore, it's advisable to regularly review your surveillance policies and technologies. As privacy norms evolve and new technologies emerge, periodic assessments can help you stay aligned with best practices and public expectations.

Another ethical practice is the use of anonymisation techniques where feasible. For example, software that blurs faces in video footage can be employed in certain contexts to enhance privacy while still maintaining security. This approach can be particularly relevant in sensitive areas where the identification of individuals is not necessary for the intended security purpose.

Community Relations and Transparency

Finally, your approach to security and privacy extends beyond the confines of your property. It encompasses how you engage with the wider community. Transparent and open communication about your security practices can alleviate public concerns and build trust. For instance, if you are implementing a new security system that affects the surrounding area, consider hosting a community meeting to explain the measures and address any concerns.

Moreover, engaging with local privacy advocates and regulatory bodies can provide valuable insights that help refine your practices. These relationships can also position you as a responsible business leader who values civic engagement and ethical practices.

In conclusion, navigating the ethical landscape in commercial property security isn't just about mitigating risks—it's about doing so in a way that respects individual rights and fosters trust. By addressing these ethical and privacy concerns head-on, you not only protect your assets but also cultivate a secure and respectful environment that can thrive in an increasingly scrutinised world. Remember, in the realm of security, how you protect is just as important as what you protect.

RECAP AND ACTION ITEMS

You've just navigated the intricate web of legal and compliance considerations critical to operating secure commercial properties in high-stakes industries. Understanding these elements is not just about ticking boxes; it's about building a fortress that is robust yet compliant, secure yet accessible.

With the complexities of building regulations and standards under your belt, you are now equipped to ensure your property meets local and national security regulations, fire safety, accessibility requirements, and environmental impact considerations. It's vital to regularly review these regulations as they get updated and ensure your property remains compliant.

Moving onto insurance and liability, you've grasped the importance of tailoring your insurance to cover the unique risks associated with your industry. Your property's design isn't just about aesthetics or functionality—it's a powerful tool in managing liability. Consider consulting with a design expert who specializes in high-risk properties to minimise potential legal battles and enhance security features.

Lastly, the delicate balance between implementing robust security measures and respecting privacy rights cannot be overlooked. Your approach to surveillance, data protection, and community relations should be transparent and ethical. Open dialogue with your community and stakeholders about your security practices can foster trust and mitigate concerns regarding privacy infringement.

Action Steps:

1. Review and Update Compliance: Regularly check that your property complies with the latest local and national regulations. A yearly review with a legal consultant can keep you on track

2. Audit Your Insurance Coverage: Annually review your insurance policies with a broker who understands the specific needs and risks of your industry. This ensures your coverage evolves with your business and regulatory changes

3. Design with Liability in Mind: Engage a security design consultant to assess your property's current layout and systems. Implement design changes that could reduce liability and enhance security

4. Strengthen Community Relations: Schedule bi-annual

meetings with your local community leaders to discuss your security measures and their impact. Transparency builds trust and can ease privacy concerns

5. Ethics and Privacy Audit: Conduct an audit of your surveillance and data handling practices to ensure they align with ethical guidelines and privacy laws. Consider hiring a privacy officer if your operations involve significant data handling or surveillance.

By taking these proactive steps, you position your commercial property not just as a secure space, but as a responsible and compliant member of the industry and community. Remember, the goal is to Protect, Prevent, and Prosper.

8

FUTURE-PROOFING: STAYING AHEAD OF THREATS

"The only way to predict the future is to have power to shape the future." - Eric Hoffer

Emerging Threats and Technologies

In the fast-paced world of high-value industries, staying one step ahead in the security game isn't just wise; it's essential. Whether you're safeguarding a bustling software development firm, a meticulous legal practice, or a busy accounting firm, understanding the landscape of emerging threats and the latest defensive technologies can make all the difference. Let's delve into the dynamics of anticipating future security challenges, explore innovations in defensive technologies, and unpack global trends in security threats.

Anticipating Future Security Challenges

Imagine you're playing a high-stakes game of chess. Every move you make is about predicting and countering your opponent's next steps. Similarly, in the realm of security, anticipating challenges is paramount. As technology evolves, so do the methods by which your commercial property can be compromised.

Cyber threats are a rapidly growing concern. For industries dealing with sensitive data—be it game development codes or confidential legal documents—the digital doorway is often targeted. Ransomware attacks, where your data is held hostage, and phishing scams that seek to sneak through your digital defences are on the rise. Moreover, the integration of IoT (Internet of Things) devices in commercial properties introduces new vulnerabilities. These connected devices can offer convenience and efficiency but can also serve as entry points for cyberattacks.

Physical security threats are also evolving. The use of drones for surveillance or delivery is becoming commonplace, and they could be used for nefarious purposes, such as scouting out vulnerabilities in your property's physical security or even direct attacks.

Staying ahead means not just reacting to these threats, but anticipating them. This involves regular risk assessments and staying attuned to the advancements in technology that may affect your security strategy.

Innovations in Defensive Technologies

As threats evolve, so do the means to counter them. Innovations in defensive technologies are not just about keeping unwanted guests out, but also about managing and mitigating risks in smarter, more efficient ways.

Let's talk about cybersecurity innovations first. AI and machine learning are revolutionising how security systems understand and react to threats. These technologies can analyse patterns, predict potential breaches, and automate responses at speeds and accuracies far beyond human capabilities. For instance, AI-driven security platforms can monitor your network traffic in real time, detecting anomalies that could indicate a breach and responding instantly to neutralise threats.

On the physical front, biometric security systems are becoming more sophisticated. Beyond fingerprint scanning, facial recognition and iris scanning technologies are being integrated into access control systems. These systems offer a higher level of security, reducing the risk of unauthorised access through stolen or lost access cards.

Moreover, smart surveillance technologies equipped with real-time analytics can now identify unusual behaviours and alert security personnel instantly. These systems use complex algorithms to distinguish between routine movements and potential security threats, such as someone loitering near entry points or unauthorised attempts to access restricted areas.

Global Trends in Security Threats

Understanding global trends in security threats is crucial for fortifying your defences against not only local but also international risks. In our interconnected world, a security breach in one part of the globe can ripple across to your doorstep.

Data breaches and cyberattacks are among the most significant global trends affecting commercial properties. With more businesses storing sensitive information digitally, the incentive for cybercriminals to breach these virtual vaults is skyrocketing. The international nature of the internet means that an attack can come from anywhere, at any time.

Terrorism and organised crime also pose serious threats. These groups often target high-value industries to fund their activities or make political statements. Physical security measures, therefore, need to be robust and adaptable to counter these severe threats.

Climate change is influencing global security trends too. Natural disasters, driven by climate change, can pose indirect security risks. For instance, the chaos following a natural disaster can lead to looting or unauthorised access to properties when the usual security measures fail due to power outages or physical damages.

By keeping an eye on these global trends and understanding how they can influence local security needs, you can better prepare and protect your assets.

Navigating the complex landscape of emerging threats and technologies in security requires a proactive approach. By anticipating future challenges, leveraging new defensive technologies, and understanding global trends, you can not only protect your commercial property but also give yourself peace of mind, knowing you're prepared for whatever comes your way.

Sustainable Security Solutions

Eco-friendly Materials and Practices

In today's world, where climate change and environmental sustainability are at the forefront of global discussions, it's essential that every industry plays its part. This is no different for the security sector, especially for commercial properties in high-value industries. Adopting eco-friendly materials and practices is not just about reducing your carbon footprint; it's about setting a standard and protecting your assets in the most responsible manner.

For starters, consider the physical materials used in your security infrastructure. The development and use of biodegradable or recycled materials in the manufacturing of security devices are emerging trends. These materials not only reduce the environmental impact but also often offer enhanced durability and efficiency. For instance, biodegradable cable sheathing can be used in your electronic security systems, which reduces the amount of plastic waste generated during upgrades or replacements.

Lighting plays a crucial role in security, particularly in deterring intruders and enhancing video surveillance. Opting for LED lighting, which consumes significantly less energy than traditional bulbs, can cut down your energy consumption drastically. Solar-powered lights are another excellent option, providing reliable illumination without tapping into the grid, thus promoting energy independence.

Water usage often goes unnoticed in discussions about sustainable security practices. Yet, the integration of water-efficient landscaping around your property can contribute both to aesthetic appeal and environmental conservation. Using native plants that require minimal watering and attention can reduce your property's water use and by extension, lower the operational costs.

Sustainability in Security Design

Designing a sustainable security system involves more than just selecting the right materials; it involves integrating these systems into your property in a way that compliments your business's operational efficiency and environmental goals. The architecture of sustainability in security requires careful consideration of both form and function.

When planning the layout of your security infrastructure, think about how natural elements can assist in protecting your property. For example, strategic placement of trees and shrubs can provide natural barriers that are both aesthetically pleasing and effective in managing site security. Moreover, these natural elements can help regulate the building's temperature, reducing reliance on heating and cooling systems.

The concept of 'passive security' is worth exploring. This involves designing the building in such a way that it naturally minimises risks, thereby reducing the need for active security measures. Features like window placements being away from easy access points or having reception areas designed as natural surveillance spots can significantly enhance your security strategy while keeping it inherently sustainable.

Energy management systems can also play a pivotal role in a sustainable security design. Smart systems that integrate your security setup with your energy management can help reduce costs and environmental impact. For instance, motion sensors not only help in security but can also control lighting, heating, and cooling based on room occupancy, which reduces unnecessary energy usage.

Long-term Cost-effectiveness of Green Solutions

The initial investment in green security solutions might seem daunting compared to traditional methods. However, the long-term savings and benefits often outweigh the initial costs. Reduced operational costs, enhanced corporate reputation, and compliance with environmental regulations are just some of the benefits that come with green solutions.

Energy-efficient systems reduce utility bills. Over time, the savings from lower energy and water usage can be significant. Additionally, using durable, sustainable materials can decrease the frequency and cost of replacements and repairs. This not only saves money but also reduces the downtime and disruption that come with maintenance work.

There's also an increasingly important aspect of corporate social responsibility (CSR). By implementing sustainable practices, your business can enhance its reputation, which is crucial in high-value industries. Clients and consumers are becoming more environmentally conscious and are likely to support businesses that demonstrate a commitment to sustainability. This can translate into increased trust and loyalty, ultimately impacting your bottom line positively.

Moreover, governments and local authorities are beginning to offer incentives for businesses that take steps towards sustainability. These can come in the form of tax breaks, subsidies, or support in achieving green certifications, all of which can provide financial relief and public relations boosts.

Incorporating sustainable security solutions into your commercial property not only aids in protecting your physical assets but also aligns your business with broader global trends towards sustainability and responsibility. By choosing eco-friendly materials, designing with sustainability in mind, and understanding the cost-effectiveness of these choices, you are not just future-proofing against security threats but also against environmental and economic shifts. This strategic approach allows you to protect, prevent, and indeed prosper in a world that increasingly values green, sustainable practices.

Continuous Improvement and Adaptation

Staying Informed and Proactive

In the fast-paced world of commercial property management, resting on your laurels isn't an option. Tomorrow's security landscape will look nothing like todays, and staying one step ahead requires a proactive approach. You need to be vigilant, always scouting the horizon for new developments that could affect your security posture.

Start by making it a habit to monitor a variety of sources for the latest security news and updates. This could range from trade publications and security blogs to newsletters from industry leaders. The goal here is not just to skim through these resources but to engage deeply with the content to understand how emerging threats might impact your specific context. For instance, if you own a legal practice, changes in data protection laws could significantly affect how you need to manage and secure client information.

Moreover, technology doesn't stand still, and neither should you. Advances in AI, for instance, could offer new ways to enhance building security, from smarter surveillance systems to more effective access controls. However, these technologies also bring new vulnerabilities. Hackers are perpetually in the loop, adapting their methods as technology evolves. By staying informed, you pre-emptively adjust your security strategies and implement necessary upgrades before potential breaches can occur.

Regular Training and Updates

Knowledge is a critical asset, but it's only powerful if it's current. Regular training and updates for yourself and your staff are essential to maintain a fortress-like facade. This doesn't mean dragging everyone through a tedious annual seminar. Instead, integrate training into your regular operations in engaging, manageable segments.

Consider implementing quarterly security workshops that focus on different aspects of your security setup. These could cover everything from physical security drills to cyber hygiene practices, depending on what's most relevant for your industry. For instance, a game development studio might focus on intellectual property security and protecting against data breaches, while an accounting firm might concentrate on compliance with financial data protection standards.

Training should also include simulations of potential security incidents to ensure everyone knows how to react under pressure. These exercises reinforce theoretical knowledge and help to iron out any kinks in your emergency response strategies.

Additionally, make use of online platforms for ongoing education. Many cybersecurity firms offer webinars and online courses that could be beneficial. Encourage your staff to participate in these sessions by offering incentives such as recognition or small bonuses for those who complete them.

Engaging with Security Communities

No commercial property owner is an island, especially when it comes to security. Engaging with broader security communities can provide invaluable insights and support. These communities range from local business groups to international security organizations, providing a plethora of opportunities for connection and learning.

Start by identifying relevant security networks that align with your industry's specific needs. For example, if you're in the software development industry, look for tech-centric security groups that discuss and tackle issues like software piracy or digital espionage. Participation in these groups can be as simple as joining a forum or attending regular meet-ups.

Networking in these communities isn't just about receiving; it's also about giving back. Sharing your own experiences and solutions can establish you as a thought leader in your niche, enhancing your reputation and potentially leading to collaborative opportunities that could bolster your security measures further.

Furthermore, consider partnering with local law enforcement and private security firms. These entities often have a wealth of experience and resources that can provide specific insights or assistance. They may offer programs or workshops that can benefit your understanding and preparedness for dealing with both common and sophisticated threats.

Lastly, don't underestimate the power of technology in fostering community engagement. Platforms like LinkedIn allow you to connect with security professionals globally, enabling you to exchange knowledge and stay updated on global security trends that might eventually impact your local operations.

By continuously engaging with these communities, you not only keep your finger on the pulse of the latest security developments but also build a support network that can be crucial in times of crisis.

In conclusion, adapting to the ever-changing security environment requires a dynamic, informed approach. By staying informed, regularly updating and training your team, and engaging actively with security communities, you ensure that your commercial properties are not just protected for today but are also prepared for the threats of tomorrow. This continuous cycle of improvement and adaptation is essential in maintaining a secure environment that supports your business's growth and resilience.

RECAP AND ACTION ITEMS

FUTURE-PROOFING: STAYING AHEAD OF THREATS

Congratulations on navigating through the intricacies of future-proofing your commercial properties! You've now armed yourself with knowledge on emerging security threats and technologies, embraced the principles of sustainable security solutions, and understood the importance of continuous improvement and adaptation. The road ahead is clear; it's time to put these strategies into practice and stay ahead of the curve.

Firstly, take a moment to reflect on the key technologies and trends identified. How might these impact your specific industry, whether it's software development, legal services, or accounting? Begin by conducting a risk assessment tailored to these insights. This isn't just a one-off task; make it a regular part of your annual review. Remember, the goal is to anticipate and mitigate risks before they materialise.

Next, let's talk sustainability. It's not just good for the planet; it's smart business too. Evaluate your current security measures and materials. Where can you integrate eco-friendly alternatives? This might mean upgrading to energy-efficient security systems or adopting biodegradable materials for physical barriers. Also, consider the design of your security measures. Are they adaptable to changes, or will they require complete overhauls as technology evolves? Aim for modularity and flexibility.

Investing in green solutions can seem costly upfront, but remember their long-term cost-effectiveness. They often pay for themselves through lower operational costs and potential tax incentives. Make a plan to phase these into your business, starting with the most feasible and impactful.

Finally, you cannot underestimate the power of community and continuous learning. Join forums, attend webinars, and network with other professionals in your field. The collective wisdom of a community can provide insights and foresight that go beyond individual experience. Ensure your staff are regularly trained on both the tools and tactics they need to remain vigilant against new threats.

By following these steps, you're not just protecting your assets; you're setting a benchmark in your industry for responsibility and foresight. Keep pushing the boundaries, stay informed, and remain proactive. Your business isn't just surviving; it's thriving, securely and sustainably.

9

CASE STUDIES OF SECURED BUILDINGS

"Distrust and caution are the parents of security." - Benjamin Franklin

Lessons from the Front Lines

Analysis of Successful Security Implementations

In the world of high-value commercial properties, the line between vulnerability and security is often defined by the robustness of implemented measures. Consider the scenario of a leading software game developer located in the bustling heart of London. With intellectual property worth millions and a constant flow of digital traffic, their security strategy needed to be watertight. The company opted for a multi-layered security approach that integrated advanced cybersecurity measures with physical security enhancements.

One standout feature was the use of biometric authentication to access their main development floors. This wasn't just any fingerprint scanner; it was a state-of-the-art system capable of detecting blood flow and heart rate to ensure that the person entering was not under duress. Additionally, all data traffic in and out of the building was routed through encrypted channels, with AI-driven behaviour analytics to flag any unusual activities instantly.

The key takeaway here? Don't just settle for generic solutions. Tailoring your security measures to address specific vulnerabilities can significantly fortify your fortress against both physical and digital threats.

Key Takeaways from Failed Security Measures

Transitioning from triumphs to teachable moments, let's dissect a less fortunate incident involving a high-profile legal firm in Manchester. The firm had invested heavily in what appeared to be a robust CCTV system. However, the devil was in the details—or rather, the lack thereof. The cameras installed offered excellent visual quality but were positioned in such a way that crucial entry and exit points were left unmonitored. This oversight provided an exploitable blind spot for a well-coordinated break-in.

Moreover, the firm had underestimated the need for integrating their physical and digital security measures. The intruders accessed client files through a workstation left logged in overnight, an avoidable mistake had there been stricter access controls and employee training.

From this debacle, the crucial lesson is clear: Comprehensive security is not just about having the right tools but also about meticulous implementation and regular audits to ensure no stone is left unturned.

Comparative Studies of Similar Risk Profiles

To encapsulate the essence of tailored security strategies further, let's compare two accountancy firms, both situated in high-risk areas in Glasgow but with differing approaches to security.

Firm A adopted a relatively standard security protocol, featuring basic alarm systems and standard lock-and-key access to their premises. Firm B, on the other hand, decided to integrate advanced security technologies, including motion sensors, high-definition surveillance cameras, and electronic access control systems with personalised key codes for each employee.

Over a span of two years, Firm A faced two break-ins, which resulted in significant financial losses and elevated insurance premiums. Firm B, with its proactive approach, experienced no such incidents; the sophisticated security system not only deterred potential burglaries but also instilled a greater sense of security among the staff, which in turn boosted workplace productivity.

This comparative analysis underscores a pivotal point: Investing in advanced, customised security solutions can yield dividends, not just by protecting assets but also by enhancing overall business operations.

Innovations in Action

Breakthrough technologies and how they were applied

In the realm of commercial property security, staying ahead of the curve isn't just advisable; it's imperative. Let's dive into how some trailblazing technologies have been harnessed to secure high-value commercial properties like yours, setting new standards in the industry.

Take, for example, the integration of facial recognition technology at a leading software game developer's headquarters in London. By replacing traditional key card entry systems, the company managed to enhance security without sacrificing speed of access for its employees. The system uses real-time facial recognition algorithms that not only improve security by preventing unauthorised access but also track the movement of individuals within the building, flagging any unusual patterns. The technology was seamlessly integrated into their existing security framework, demonstrating that adopting cutting-edge solutions doesn't always require an overhaul of current systems.

Another breakthrough came in the form of intelligent surveillance solutions. A high-profile legal firm in Manchester adopted AI-driven CCTV cameras that could differentiate between routine activities and potential security threats. These cameras use behavioural analytics to alert security personnel about specific incidents, reducing the number of false alarms and enabling a quicker response to real threats. The firm reported a significant reduction in security incidents within the first six months of implementation, proving the efficacy of smart surveillance.

Custom security solutions for unique challenges

Every commercial property comes with its own set of security challenges, necessitating bespoke solutions that cater specifically to its needs. For instance, an accounting firm located in a high-risk area in Birmingham faced frequent attempts of physical break-ins. To combat this, the firm installed a state-of-the-art intrusion detection system that utilises vibration sensors and pressure mats. These are installed around the perimeter and near all potential entry points, detecting any attempt to force entry and instantly alerting local authorities and security personnel.

Moreover, considering the confidential nature of their work, a bespoke cybersecurity solution was also implemented. This included end-to-end encryption of their internal communications and the installation of an advanced firewall that monitors data traffic for any unusual activity. The dual approach of physical and cyber protection tailored to their specific risks exemplifies how customised security measures can provide comprehensive protection.

Another unique challenge was faced by a high-end game developer in Edinburgh, whose workstations contained sensitive, unreleased game content. The risk of intellectual property theft was mitigated by a custom-designed secure access system that restricted access to specific areas of the building based on the employee's role and clearance level. Specialised encryption software was also installed on their workstations to protect against data breaches, ensuring that their creative assets remained under wraps until officially released.

Integration of aesthetics and function

Securing a commercial property doesn't mean compromising on its aesthetic appeal. Many high-value commercial properties have embraced the challenge of integrating sophisticated security features with elegant design elements.

Consider the case of a newly designed accountant's office in Bristol, which features a stunning glass façade. To maintain this design while enhancing security, the glass was treated with a transparent, bullet-resistant film. This film not only ensures high-level security but also protects against UV rays, thereby preserving the interiors from sun damage. The external appearance remains sleek and inviting, while offering the necessary resilience against potential threats.

Lighting, often overlooked, plays a crucial role in both aesthetics and security. An architectural firm in Glasgow adopted an innovative approach by integrating motion-activated floodlights into the landscape design. These lights are aesthetically placed within the gardens surrounding the building and are programmed to illuminate the area effectively if unusual activity is detected at night. This approach not only deters potential intruders but also enhances the building's nighttime appearance, blending functionality with visual appeal.

Lastly, the integration of green walls along with security checkpoints at the entrance of a legal practice in London showcases another excellent example of aesthetics meeting function. The green walls serve as a natural air filter and create a calming entrance for clients and employees, while the checkpoints ensure that everyone entering the building is authorised and recorded without creating a 'fortress-like' feel.

Through these examples, it's clear that innovation in securing commercial properties not only focuses on adopting new technologies but also on customising solutions to meet unique challenges and integrating them with aesthetic elements to create environments that are secure, functional, and inviting. As you consider the security measures for your own properties, think about how you can apply these innovative ideas to ensure protection without compromising on style or functionality.

Global Examples of Excellence

Security Design in Different Cultural Contexts

Venturing beyond your local shores, let's take a global tour to understand how cultural contexts shape security designs in commercial properties. Each region brings its own set of values, traditions, and environmental challenges that influence security measures, making this a rich field for learning and application.

In Japan, for instance, the concept of *Omotenashi*, which translates to selfless hospitality, permeates not just service industries but also how they secure their premises. Rather than glaring cameras and overt security personnel, many Japanese firms integrate security within their customer service protocols. Subtle yet sophisticated, these measures include biometric authenticators in entryways camouflaged within digital reception desks, offering a seamless blend of hospitality and security.

Switching gears to the Middle East, particularly the UAE, where the aesthetic integration into security design is paramount, you find that the cultural emphasis on opulence and modernity demands that security devices not only perform effectively but also complement the luxurious façade of their buildings. Advanced surveillance systems are often hidden in ornamental features, and robust access controls are installed in such a way that they accentuate the architectural beauty rather than detract from it.

In Nordic countries, with their deep-rooted values of trust and openness, security solutions focus on transparency and inclusivity. There, it's common to find open-access lobbies with visible, yet unobtrusive, security measures. These include advanced yet aesthetically fitting surveillance cameras and community-focused security apps that allow for real-time updates and alerts, fostering a collective responsibility for security.

Adaptations to Local Threats and Regulations

Delving into how commercial properties adapt to local threats and regulatory frameworks across the globe can offer you actionable insights. For instance, in earthquake-prone areas like California or Japan, commercial buildings are not only structurally designed to withstand tremors but also incorporate security features that ensure swift evacuation and immediate emergency communication, tailored to such natural threats.

In contrast, in places like South Africa where commercial crime rates are high, businesses often incorporate multi-layered physical security measures. These might include perimeter walls topped with electric fences, monitored by CCTV cameras that link directly to armed response teams. Here, the regulatory environment allows, and indeed sometimes necessitates, more visible and assertive security measures than might be acceptable in other parts of the world.

European Union data protection laws, such as the GDPR, also

significantly influence security strategies for buildings housing businesses like legal practices or software developers. In these cases, cybersecurity is as crucial as physical security. Commercial buildings in such regions often serve as fortresses of data protection, with biometric access controls and encrypted communication systems that ensure both compliance and security.

Inspirational Stories of Resilience and Recovery

Lastly, let's draw some inspiration from stories of resilience and recovery in the face of adversities—because sometimes, security isn't just about prevention but also about bouncing back with strength.

Take the example of a major gaming software company in California that experienced a severe data breach. The breach not only threatened their intellectual property but also their reputation. However, using this crisis as a catalyst, the company overhauled its security protocols completely, integrating state-of-the-art cybersecurity measures along with enhanced physical security strategies. The recovery involved not just technological upgrades but also a cultural shift towards more stringent security practices, turning a potential disaster into a testament to resilience and proactive leadership.

Then there's the story from Tokyo, post-2011 earthquake and tsunami. A multi-tenant building housing several high-value tech firms was severely damaged. However, the swift activation of well-practiced emergency protocols saved countless lives, and the subsequent rebuilding incorporated advanced seismic technologies, making it one of the safest—and most inspiring—commercial buildings in the region.

These examples not only serve as lessons in the face of challenges but also resonate as beacons of hope and determination, demonstrating that with the right measures and mindset, recovery and resilience are always within reach.

Drawing from these global exemplars, you can see how deeply cultural nuances, local threats, and inspirational resilience can influence and enhance security strategies. Each example provides a blueprint that can be adapted and applied, ensuring that your commercial property doesn't just survive in its environment but thrives securely and prosperously.

RECAP AND ACTION ITEMS

You've just navigated through a series of compelling case studies on securing commercial properties, extracting vital lessons from both successes and failures, and exploring innovative security solutions tailored to high-stakes environments. Now, it's time to convert these insights into tangible actions that protect your assets and foster a prosperous business environment.

1. Conduct a Thorough Risk Assessment: Start by understanding the unique threats relevant to your industry and location. Whether you are a game developer with intellectual property risks or a legal firm with sensitive client data, identifying these risks is the first step towards effective mitigation.

2. Benchmark Your Current Security Measures: Use the analyses from successful security implementations as a benchmark. How does your current strategy compare? Are there gaps in your physical or cyber security measures that leave you vulnerable?

3. Learn from Others' Mistakes: Reflect on the key takeaways from failed security measures. It's often cheaper to learn from others' mistakes than to make them yourself. Ensure that your security protocols are not only robust but also adaptable to changing threats.

4. Embrace Technological Innovations: Consider integrating breakthrough technologies that align with your security needs. This could range from advanced surveillance systems to AI-driven cyber defence mechanisms. Remember, the goal is not just to adopt new tech but to enhance overall security efficacy.

5. Customise Your Security Solutions: Every property has its unique challenges. Drawing inspiration from the custom solutions discussed, think about how these can be adapted or tailored to meet your specific needs without compromising on aesthetics or function.

6. Engage with Global Perspectives: The examples of excellence on a global scale highlight the importance of contextual security design. Consider how adaptations to local threats and regulations can be applied to your property, ensuring compliance and resilience.

7. Document Your Security Strategy: Finally, create a documented security strategy that includes all the elements above. This document should be regularly reviewed and updated as threats evolve or as new technologies and methodologies become available.

By acting on these steps, you position yourself not just to protect but also to thrive in an environment where security is seen as integral to business success. Remember, effective security is not a cost—it's an investment in the stability and longevity of your business. Make sure you're not just participating in the conversation about security, but leading it in your industry.

10

BUILDING YOUR SECURITY BLUEPRINT

"There is no such thing as perfect security, only varying levels of insecurity." - Salman Rushdie

Planning and Designing for Security

Starting with Security in Mind

When it comes to safeguarding your commercial property, the adage "prevention is better than cure" couldn't be more fitting. As the owner of a high-value business—be it a bustling software development firm, a prestigious legal practice, or a meticulous accounting firm—starting with security in mind is not just an option, but a necessity. This proactive approach not only mitigates risks but also embeds a culture of safety within the architectural blueprint of your enterprise.

Firstly, understand that security begins at the conceptual stage. It's essential to envision your building as a secure fortress from the get-go. Think about the potential threats specific to your industry. For instance, a game development studio might prioritise safeguarding expensive tech and intellectual property, whereas a law firm might focus more intensely on secure data storage areas to protect sensitive client information.

Incorporate security considerations into the layout and landscaping of your property. Features such as barrier-free visibility, controlled access points, and minimal external hiding spots can significantly enhance surveillance capabilities. Moreover, integrating technology like biometric access controls or advanced surveillance systems during the planning phase can be more cost-effective and less intrusive than retrofitting them later.

Lastly, consider the future scalability of your security systems. As your business grows and technologies evolve, your security infrastructure should have the capacity to adapt and expand. Planning with flexibility in mind ensures that your security measures remain robust and relevant, protecting your assets and people without hindrance to operational flow.

Engaging with Architects and Planners

Collaboration is key. Engaging with architects and planners who are not just experts in their field but are also attuned to the latest in security technologies and trends is crucial. These professionals can translate your security needs into practical architectural solutions that are as aesthetically pleasing as they are effective.

When selecting your team, look for a track record of integrating cutting-edge security measures into commercial properties. They should be able to provide you with a portfolio of projects similar in scope and challenge to yours. Additionally, they should be open to collaborating with security consultants who can offer specialised insights that architects or planners might not possess.

During the design phase, communication is your greatest tool. Regular meetings and updates can ensure that your security requirements are not only understood but also meticulously implemented. It's beneficial to involve your IT team as well, especially when the security solutions impact or integrate with your network infrastructure.

Architects and planners should also help you navigate local regulations and compliance requirements. Security features, particularly those that involve surveillance or data collection, must adhere to legal standards to avoid future liabilities.

Resources and Tools for Security Planning

Leveraging the right resources and tools can significantly streamline the security planning process. Start with industry-specific guidelines. Organisations such as the Security Industry Association (SIA) or ASIS International provide extensive resources that can guide you through the nuances of commercial property security. These resources often include risk assessment tools, best practices, and case studies that can offer valuable insights tailored to your industry.

Technology also plays a pivotal role in security planning. Advanced software tools can simulate threat scenarios and help you visualise potential security lapses in your property's design. Utilising Building Information Modelling (BIM) software not only assists in creating high-definition, scalable 3D models of your building but also integrates various data about the building's physical and functional characteristics. This can be incredibly useful for planning out security logistics and infrastructure.

Additionally, consider attending workshops and seminars focused on security in commercial architecture. These can be invaluable for staying updated on new technologies, trends, and regulatory changes. Networking with other business owners and security professionals at these events can also provide you with first-hand accounts of what works and what doesn't in real-world scenarios.

In essence, the journey to a secure commercial property begins right from the moment you start planning. By embedding security into the DNA of your property's design, engaging with the right professionals, and utilising the best available resources and tools, you can create a space that not only fosters innovation and productivity but also ensures peace of mind for you and your valued employees. Remember, in the world of high-value industries, an ounce of prevention in security planning is worth a pound of cure in potential losses.

Budgeting for Building Security

Cost Considerations and Funding Options

When it comes to securing high-value commercial properties, understanding the financial landscape is key. You're not just buying locks and cameras; you're investing in a comprehensive system that protects your assets, your employees, and your peace of mind. The cost can vary wildly based on the size of your property, the level of security you require, and the technology you choose. So, where do you start?

First, get a clear picture of what you need. This involves a risk assessment to identify potential vulnerabilities—a step you should ideally cover during the security planning phase. Once you know what you need, you can start pricing out solutions. This might range from basic CCTV systems to advanced biometric access controls. Each option comes with its own price tag and level of security.

Next, explore funding options. If upfront costs seem daunting, consider leasing equipment or financing options. Leasing can often include maintenance and upgrades, ensuring your technology never becomes obsolete. Some vendors also offer financing plans that spread the cost over time, which can help manage cash flow—crucial for maintaining the other aspects of your business.

Don't overlook the possibility of government grants and incentives, especially if your operations require heightened security measures due to the nature of your industry. These can significantly offset initial costs and make higher-end options more attainable.

Remember, investing in security is just that—an investment. It's about reducing risks that could lead to far greater losses, both financial and reputational.

Balancing Budget and Safety

Achieving the right balance between budget and safety is more art than science. It requires a strategic approach where every pound spent works towards mitigating specific risks. The goal here isn't to cut costs indiscriminately but to allocate resources in a way that maximises your return on investment in terms of security.

Start by prioritising measures that address the most critical vulnerabilities. For instance, if data theft is a significant risk, your first investment should probably be in robust cybersecurity measures before upgrading physical locks. Every industry has unique risks. For software game developers, protecting intellectual property might be paramount, whereas for legal practices, client confidentiality takes precedence.

It's also wise to consider the visibility of security measures. Visible deterrents can often prevent incidents before they begin. However, balance this with the need for subtlety in certain areas. For example, overt security measures might not be the right approach for a high-end legal firm's lobby where creating a welcoming environment is crucial.

Furthermore, consider the longevity and maintenance costs of the security measures you implement. Cheaper upfront solutions can sometimes lead to higher long-term costs due to maintenance, replacements, or less effective deterrence and protection. Opting for quality systems with good warranties and low maintenance requirements might be more cost-effective over time.

Long-term Financial Planning for Security Upgrades

Security technology evolves rapidly, driven by advances in technology and shifts in threat landscapes. What works today might become obsolete tomorrow. Therefore, it's crucial to plan not just for immediate needs but for the future.

One effective strategy is to plan for incremental upgrades. Rather than a complete overhaul every few years, consider smaller, consistent investments that keep your security state-of-the-art. This approach helps spread out costs and reduces the burden of significant one-time expenses.

Set aside a portion of your budget each year for security upgrades. Treat it as a non-negotiable expense. This fund can also cover unexpected needs, like replacing a system that's failed or upgrading earlier than planned due to a new threat.

Additionally, keep abreast of new developments in security technology. Attending industry conferences, subscribing to relevant publications, and maintaining relationships with security consultants can all provide insights into new tools and strategies that could benefit your business.

Lastly, review your security measures regularly—both in terms of their physical and functional adequacy. This not only ensures that they are functioning as intended but also that they continue to meet the security needs as your business evolves. Changes in your business, such as expansion, downsizing, or changing operational focus, all warrant a review of your security infrastructure to ensure it still aligns with your needs and risks.

By integrating these strategies into your financial planning, you ensure that your security measures remain robust and responsive to the dynamic landscape of threats, protecting your business now and in the future.

Implementing and Reviewing Security Measures

Step-by-step guide to implementing security enhancements

Embarking on the journey of enhancing your commercial property's security is no small feat. Let's break it down into manageable steps to ensure that you cover all bases without feeling overwhelmed.

Step 1: Prioritise Based on Assessment Begin with the security vulnerabilities identified during your planning phase. Prioritise these based on risk severity and potential impact on your business. For instance, if you're a software game developer, protecting your intellectual property might take precedence, necessitating advanced cybersecurity measures alongside physical security upgrades.

Step 2: Select Appropriate Technologies Choosing the right technology is crucial. Whether it's biometric access controls, advanced surveillance systems, or intrusion detection systems, ensure the solutions are scalable and integrate seamlessly with existing systems. Always opt for technologies with robust support and update policies to stay ahead of potential threats.

Step 3: Engage with Professionals For installation, don't skimp. Hire professionals with a solid track record. Their expertise can save you not only money in the long run but also ensure that your security systems function optimally. Make sure they understand the unique needs of your industry—whether it's maintaining client confidentiality in a law firm or protecting sensitive data in an accounting practice.

Step 4: Employee TrainingSecurity technology is only as effective as the people operating it. Invest in comprehensive training for your staff to handle the new systems. Regular drills and updates on security protocols can bolster your team's readiness against potential threats.

Step5: Test the Systems Before going live, rigorously test the new security measures to iron out any kinks. Simulated breaches can help identify weaknesses not apparent during the design phase. This step is crucial to ensure that when you need these systems to perform, they don't falter.

Monitoring effectiveness and making adjustments

Post-implementation, the real work begins—monitoring and adjusting. This stage is vital to ensure that the security measures you've put in place are giving you the bang for your buck.

Regular Monitoring Set up a schedule for regular checks and audits of your security systems. Use metrics and KPIs to measure effectiveness. For instance, monitor the frequency of security alerts, the response time of security personnel, and the incidence of security breaches.

Feedback Loop Create a feedback loop involving everyone from security staff to the executive team. Encourage reporting of any security lapses or flaws in the system. This inclusivity not only enhances security awareness across your enterprise but also fosters a culture of continuous improvement.

Technology Updates Security technology evolves rapidly. Keep your systems up to date with the latest software updates and hardware upgrades to fend off new threats. Regularly consult with your security technology providers about emerging tools and features that could enhance your security framework.

Adjustments Based on Evolution Your business will evolve, and so should your security measures. Whether it's through expansion, the introduction of new technology, or shifts in your operational environment, regular reviews will help adjust your security strategies to align with current business realities.

Ensuring ongoing compliance and safety

The final piece of the puzzle is compliance. Staying aligned with legal and regulatory requirements is essential for avoiding fines and reinforcing the legitimacy of your business.

Understand Legal Requirements Stay informed about the compliance standards relevant to your industry. Whether it's data protection laws for developers or confidentiality obligations for legal practices, understanding these requirements is crucial.

Regular Compliance Audits Conduct compliance audits regularly to ensure every aspect of your security measures meets industry standards and legal requirements. Consider hiring external auditors for an unbiased review of your compliance status.

Safety Protocols Beyond compliance, focus on the safety of your physical and digital environments. This includes everything from ensuring that physical safety measures are fail-proof to safeguarding against data breaches that could compromise client or employee information.

Documentation Keep thorough records of all your security protocols, audits, updates, and compliance checks. Documentation is not only crucial for regulatory purposes but also serves as a reference point in enhancing your security strategies.

Continuous Education The landscape of threats and security technology is ever-changing. Encourage continuous education and training for yourself and your team. Attend workshops, seminars, and other training sessions to stay ahead of the curve.

Implementing and reviewing security measures is a dynamic and ongoing process. By breaking it down into structured steps, monitoring outcomes, and ensuring compliance, you fortify your commercial property against existing and emerging threats. More importantly, you create a secure environment where your business can thrive without the looming worry of security lapses.

RECAP AND ACTION ITEMS

You've just taken a crucial step towards fortifying your commercial property by navigating through the comprehensive blueprint of security planning, budgeting, and implementation. Let's crystallise what you've learned into actionable steps to ensure your building is not just a workspace but a stronghold of safety and efficiency.

1. Start with Security in Mind: Revisit your initial sketches and plans. Reflect on the integration of security measures from the ground up. If you're in the initial stages, perfect! If you've already built your structure, think about how you can retrofit security elements without disrupting the essence of your existing architecture.

2. Engage with Architects and Planners: Security isn't just about cameras and alarms; it's about creating an environment that inherently deters threats. Contact professionals who understand the nuances of secure architectural design. This might mean scheduling another meeting to discuss how security can be woven into the very fabric of your property's design.

3. Utilise Resources and Tools for Security Planning: There's a wealth of information out there. Dive into the latest software and planning tools designed to simulate and predict security breaches. Utilise these tools to see where your plan stands and where it could potentially falter.

4. Budget Wisely: Security is an investment, not an expense. Review your financial allocation and ensure that it reflects the value of the assets you are protecting. Explore funding options, including insurance reductions for enhanced security measures, and consider how security investments now can reduce costs in the future.

5. Balance Budget and Safety: It's tempting to cut corners to save costs. However, remember that inadequate security can cost you much more in the long run. Strike a balance where your budget aligns with effective security strategies that don't compromise on safety.

6. Plan for the Future: The security landscape is constantly evolving. Set aside a portion of your budget for future upgrades. Technologies advance, and so do the tactics of those with ill intentions. Staying ahead means planning not just for today but for the security challenges of tomorrow.

7. Implement Security Enhancements Step-by-Step: Break down your security upgrades into manageable phases. Tackle the most critical vulnerabilities first and ensure each step is implemented thoroughly before moving on to the next.

8. Monitor and Adjust: With every new system or upgrade, monitor its effectiveness meticulously. Be prepared to make adjustments as needed. Security is not a set-and-forget solution; it requires ongoing attention and refinement.

9. Ensure Compliance and Safety: Regularly review your security measures against industry standards and legal requirements. Security compliance is not just about avoiding penalties but ensuring that your property is genuinely secure.

By systematically addressing each of these areas, you're not just protecting a building; you're safeguarding your business's future. Remember, effective security is a dynamic blend of foresight, investment, and vigilance. Now, take these steps, fortify your fortress, and let security be the cornerstone of your commercial success.

SECURING SUCCESS: EMBRACING THE FUTURE OF DEFENCE

As you turn the final pages of this journey through the multifaceted world of security, it's time to reflect on the transformative path you've embarked upon. The essence of true security goes beyond mere measures and materials; it lies in the resilience and readiness you foster within yourself and your environment. You now stand at a pivotal moment, equipped with the knowledge and strategies that can fortify not just buildings, but also the confidence and safety of those within them.

Understanding the intricacies of bulletproof glass and the robustness of structural enhancements has set a solid foundation. You've explored how to integrate bollards as a perimeter defence and how to secure interior spaces effectively. More importantly, the emphasis on training and preparedness has prepared you to anticipate and react adeptly to potential threats. This comprehensive approach ensures that you are not just reacting to risks, but proactively managing them.

However, the journey does not end here. The landscape of security is ever-evolving, and staying ahead requires continuous learning and adaptation. The strategies and technologies that seem advanced today might become obsolete tomorrow. Therefore, your commitment to keeping abreast of the latest developments and best practices is crucial. It is your proactive steps that will define the security of tomorrow.

Consider how the knowledge you've gained can be applied in various scenarios, from personal properties to business infrastructures. Each chapter has not only provided you with tools but also with the mindset to think critically about security. You have learned to assess risks, identify vulnerabilities, and implement the most effective defences. Now, it's time to put these skills into practice.

Implementing these strategies will undoubtedly bring about significant changes. You may find that your newly acquired knowledge not only enhances your physical security but also elevates your mental fortitude. Knowing that you are well-protected allows you to focus more on what truly matters in your personal and professional life.

Moreover, the human element of security—your ability to prepare and train others—cannot be overlooked. By passing on this knowledge, you empower more people to protect themselves and their communities. Security, in its truest sense, is a collective effort. When one is secure, it contributes to the safety of all.

Now, as you move forward, remember that the path to enhanced security is iterative. Each step you take builds on the previous one, creating a more robust defence system. Your journey might introduce new challenges, but with the foundation you've built, you will be ready to tackle them head-on.

If you find that the complexities of implementing these strategies are daunting, or if you seek to further your expertise, remember that help is just a click away. Whether you are looking to protect a small office or secure a large commercial complex, expert advice can provide the nuanced approach that your unique situation demands.

In conclusion, the power to enhance security lies in your hands. You've been equipped with the knowledge; now it's up to you to implement it and continue learning. Remember, the goal of security is not just to protect; it's to enable you to thrive without fear, in a space that is safeguarded against threats. Step forward with confidence, knowing that you are backed by the strongest defences, both physically and intellectually.

As you close this book, don't view it as the end of your learning journey, but as a milestone in your ongoing commitment to security and excellence. Your proactive measures will not only safeguard assets but also forge a safer future for yourself and those around you.

Together, let's build a secure, resilient, and thriving environment tailored just for you. Because when it comes to security, only the best will do, and the best is what you deserve.

www.ingramcontent.com/pod-product-compliance
Lightning Source LLC
Chambersburg PA
CBHW050101230526
45470CB00004B/1630